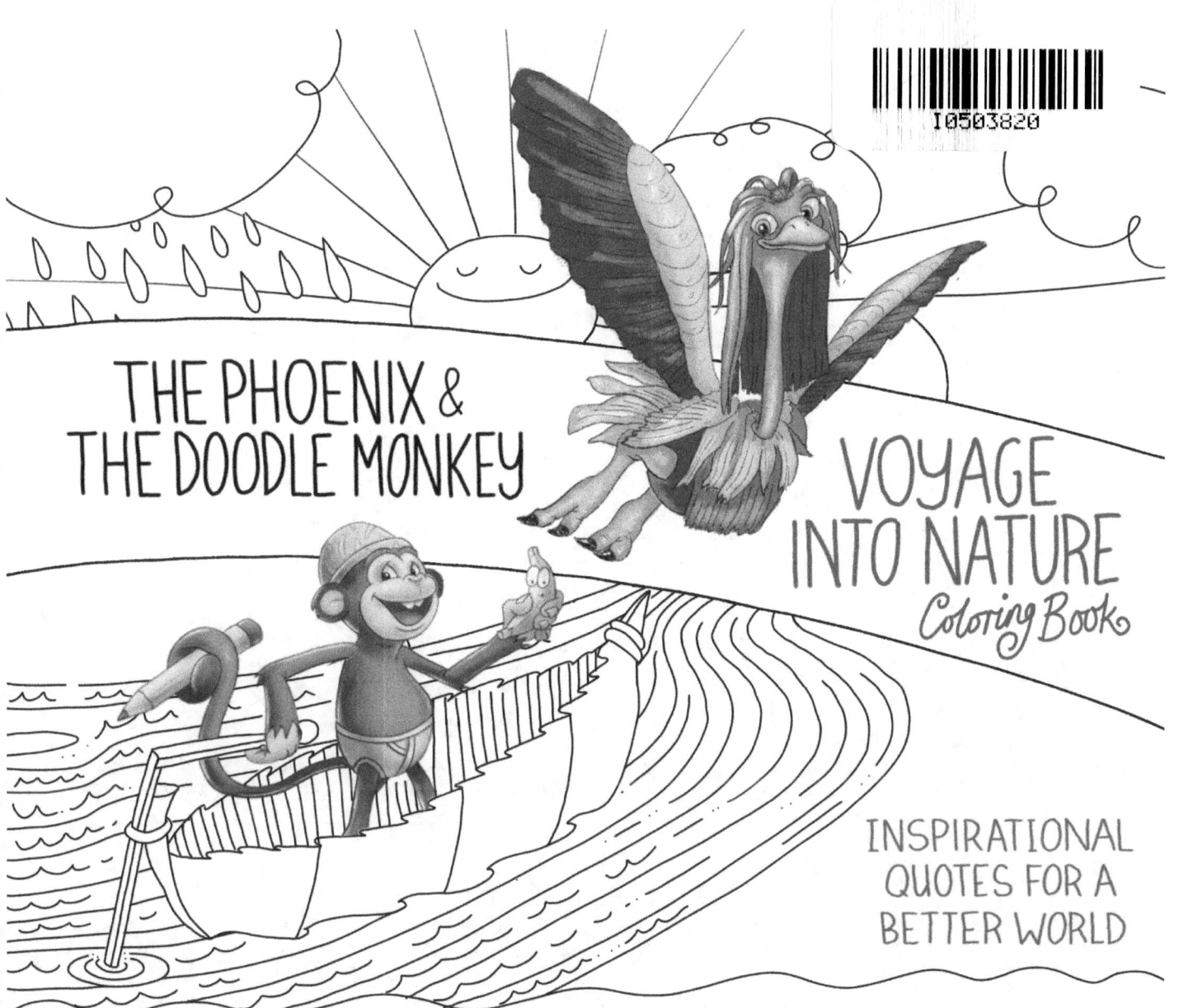

THE PHOENIX & THE DOODLE MONKEY

VOYAGE INTO NATURE
Coloring Book

INSPIRATIONAL QUOTES FOR A BETTER WORLD

I0503820

Design and Illustrations Peter Jarvis - The Doodle Monkey
Email: doodles@thedoodlemonkey.com
Web: www.thedoodlemonkey.com

Concept: Phoenix Voyage
Email: contact@phoenixvoyage.org
Web: www.phoenixvoyage.org

ISBN-13: 978-1717167323
ISBN-10: 1717167322

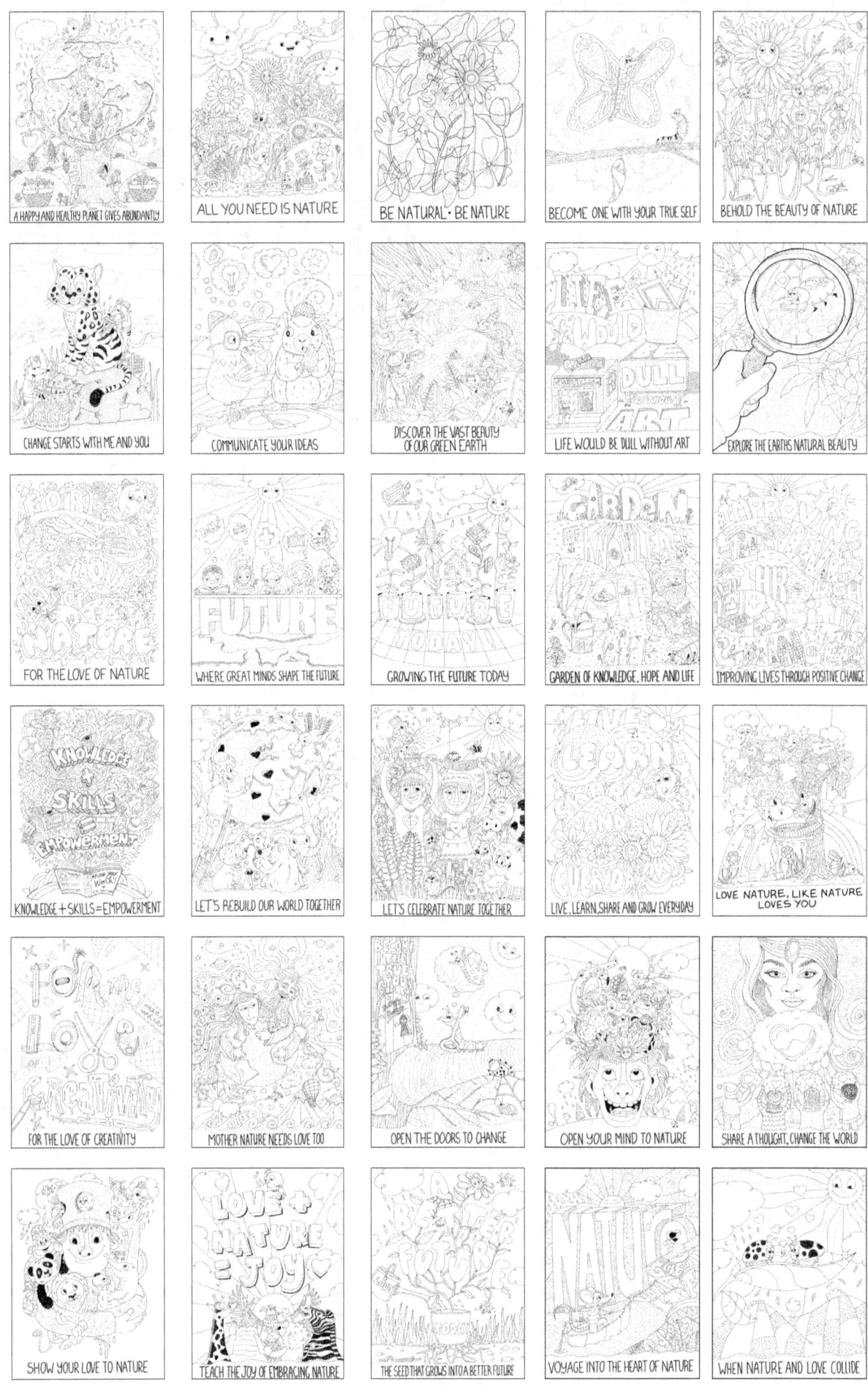

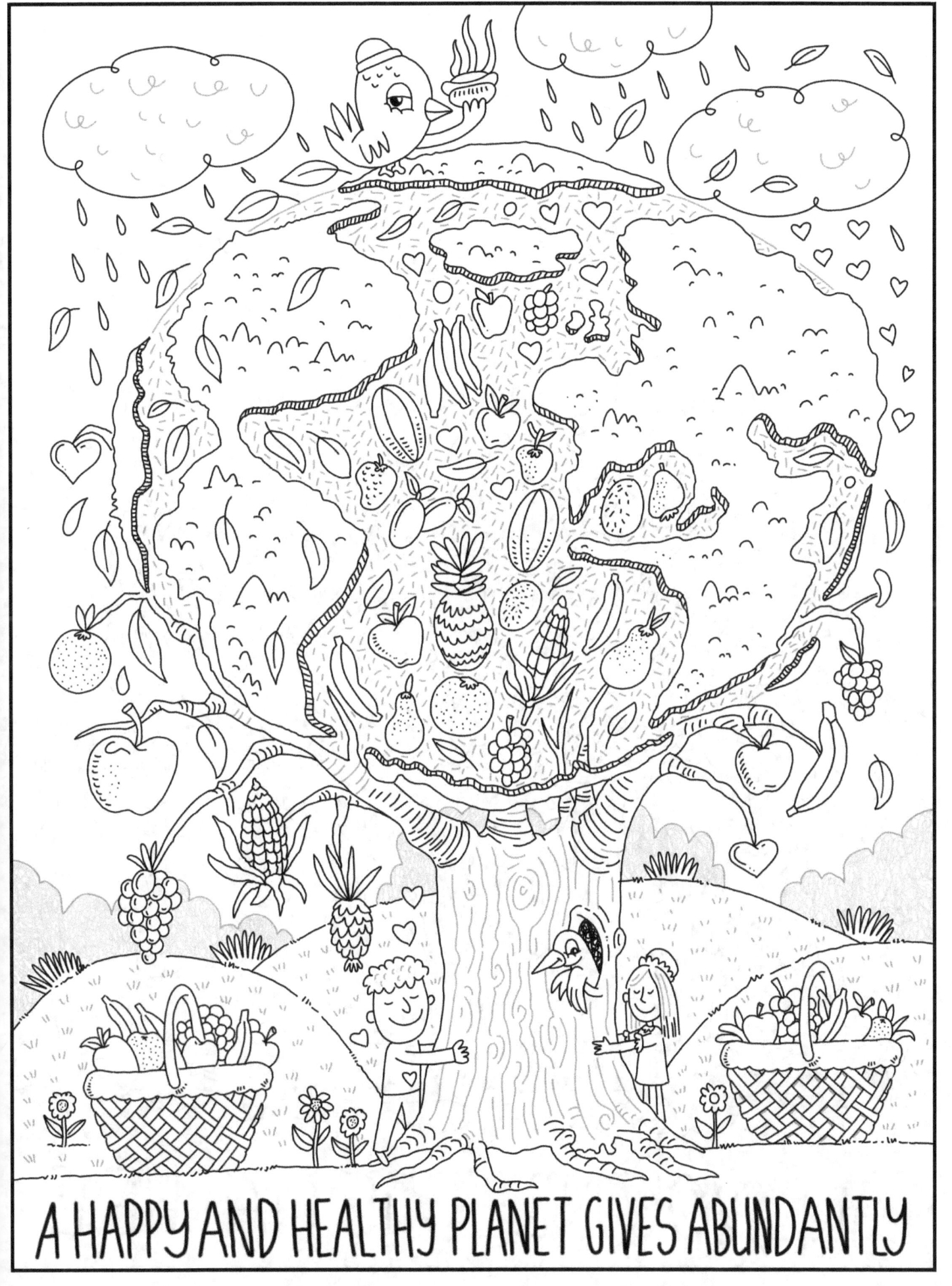

A HAPPY AND HEALTHY PLANET GIVES ABUNDANTLY

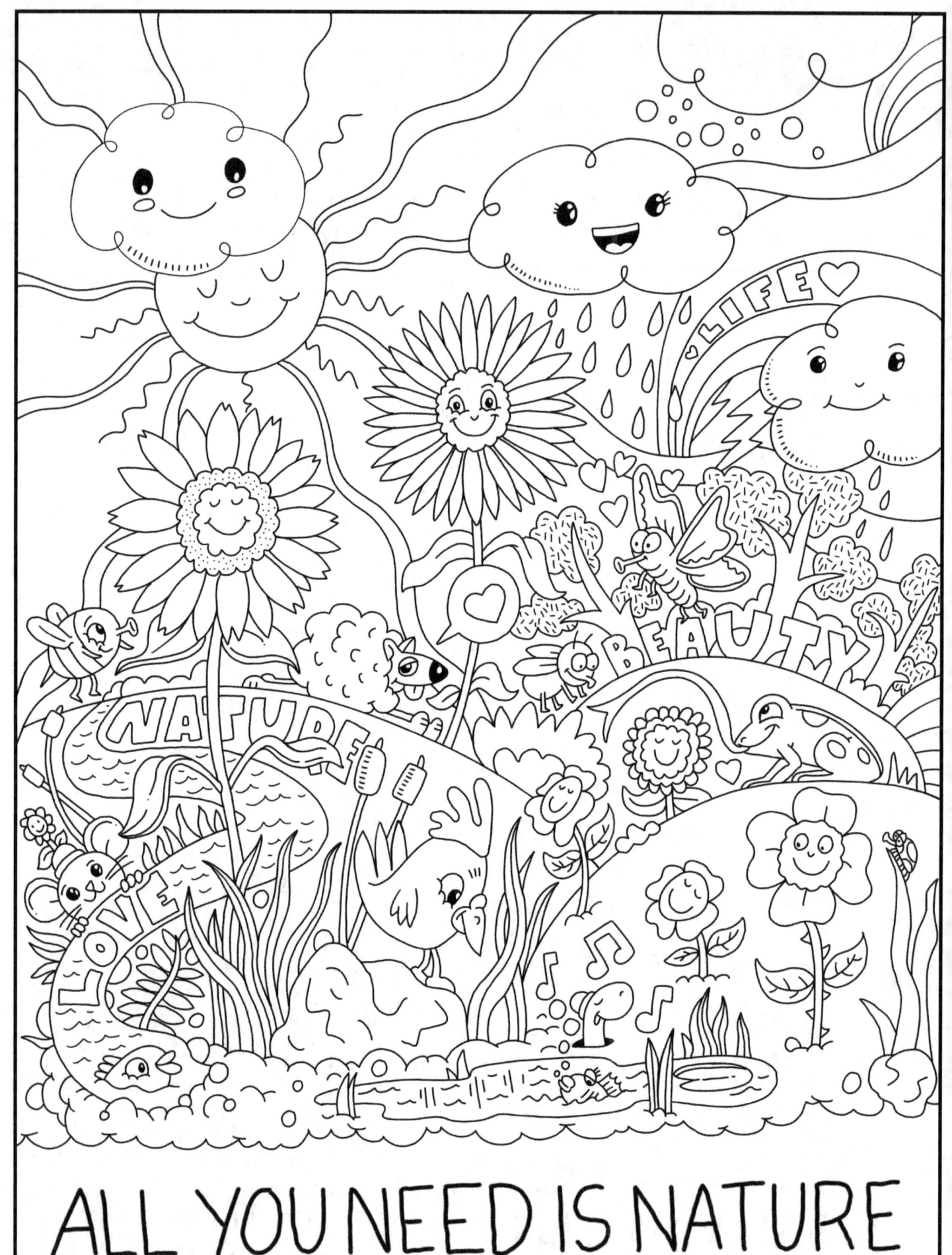

ALL YOU NEED IS NATURE

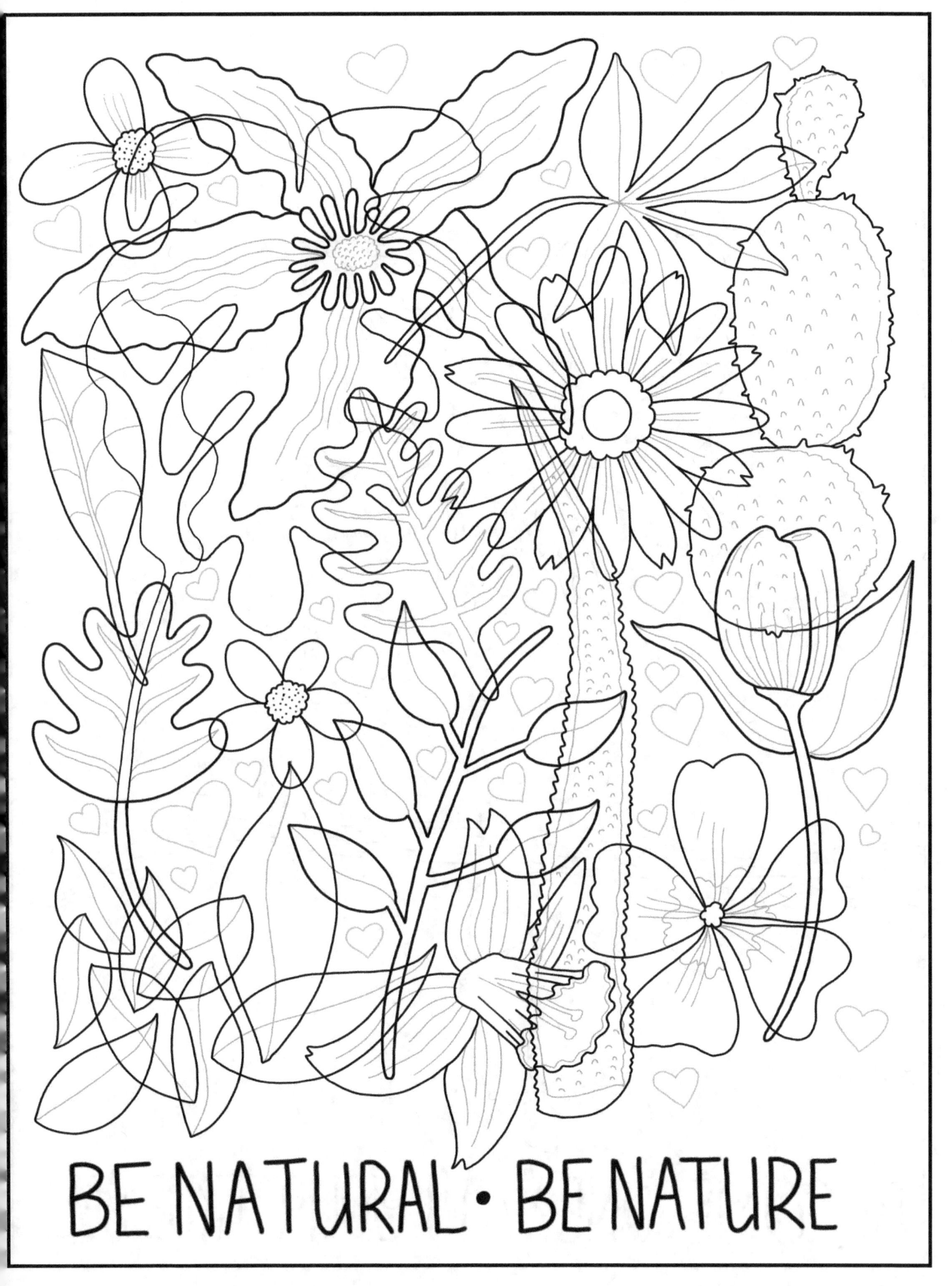

BE NATURAL • BE NATURE

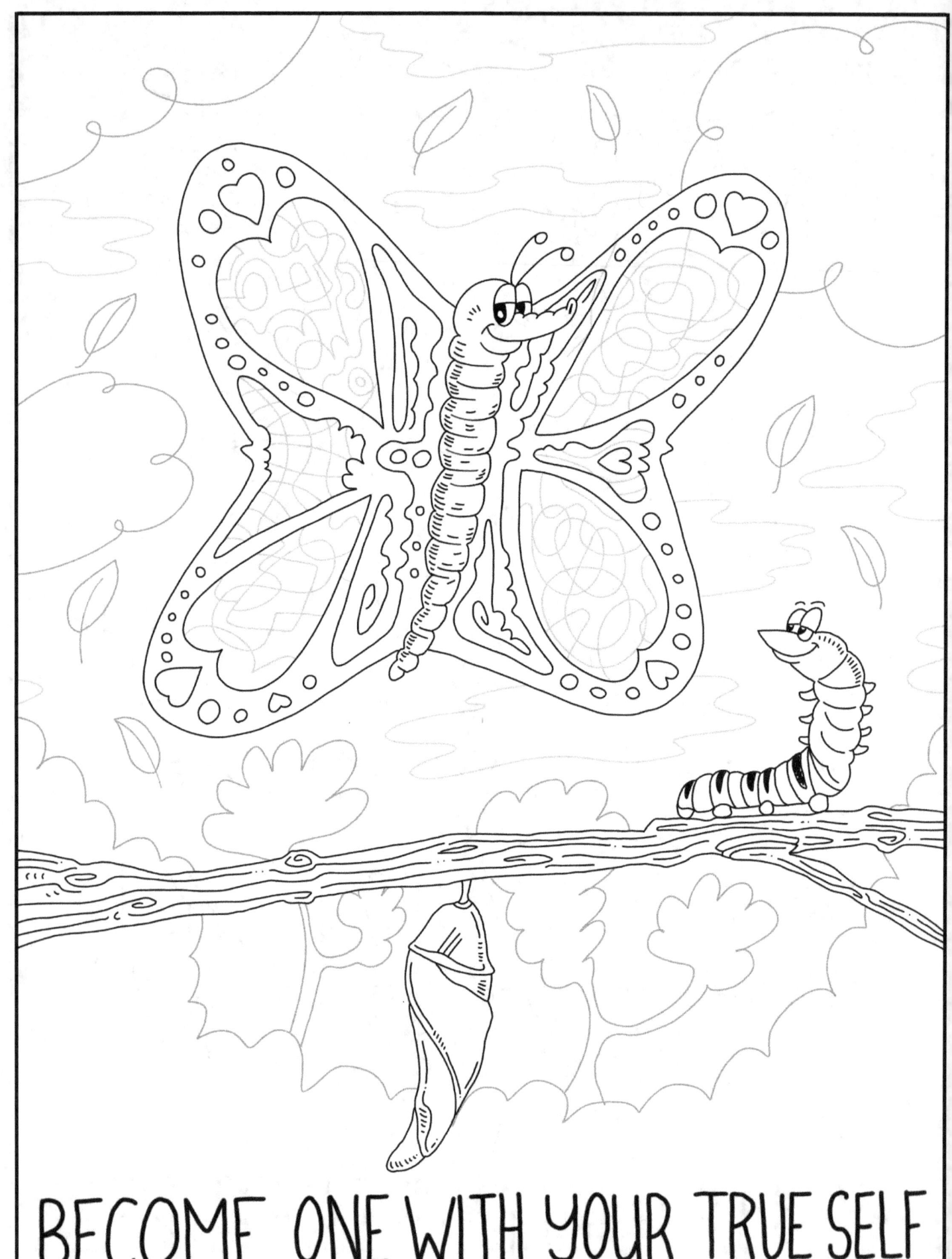

BECOME ONE WITH YOUR TRUE SELF

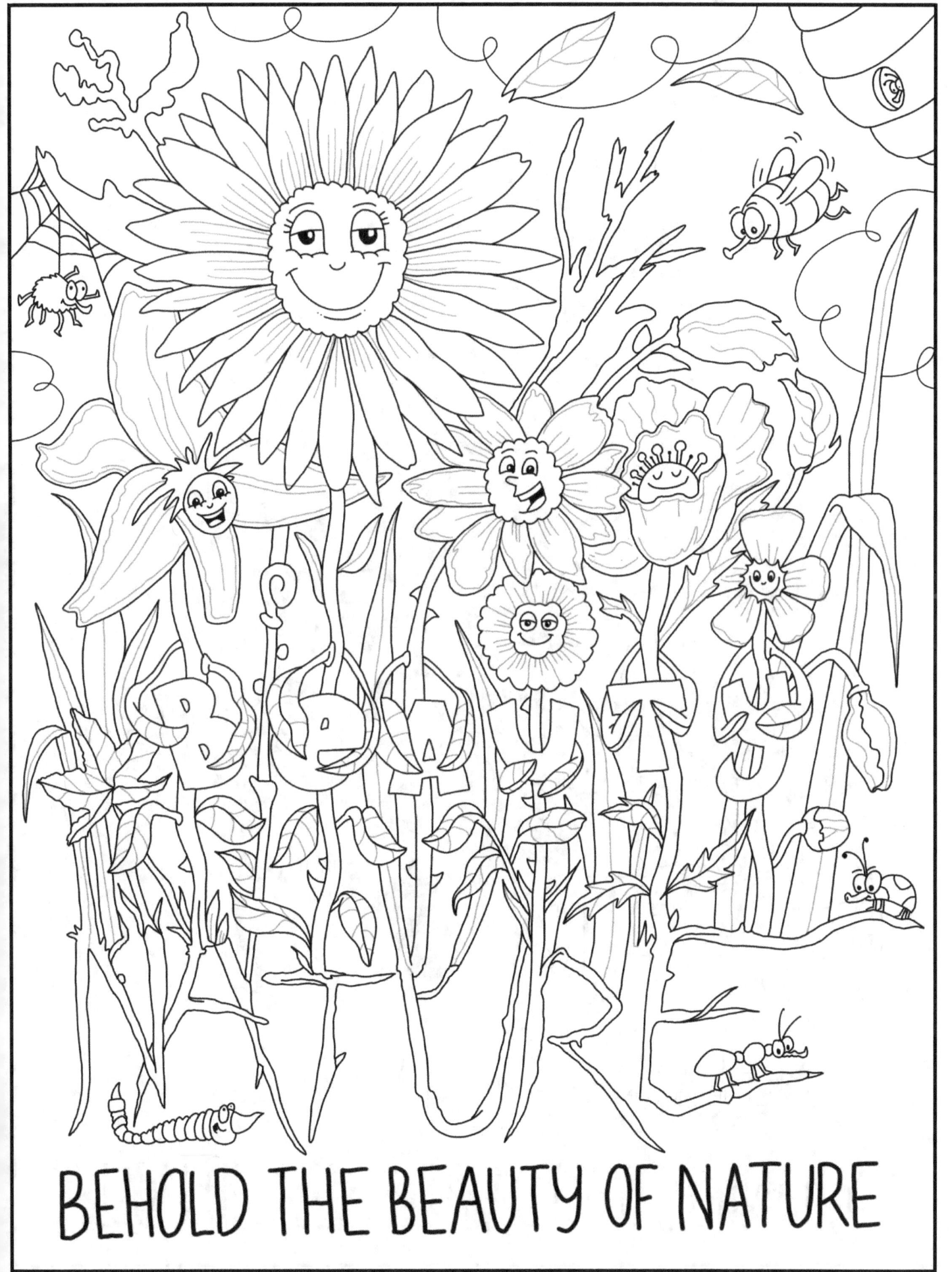

BEHOLD THE BEAUTY OF NATURE

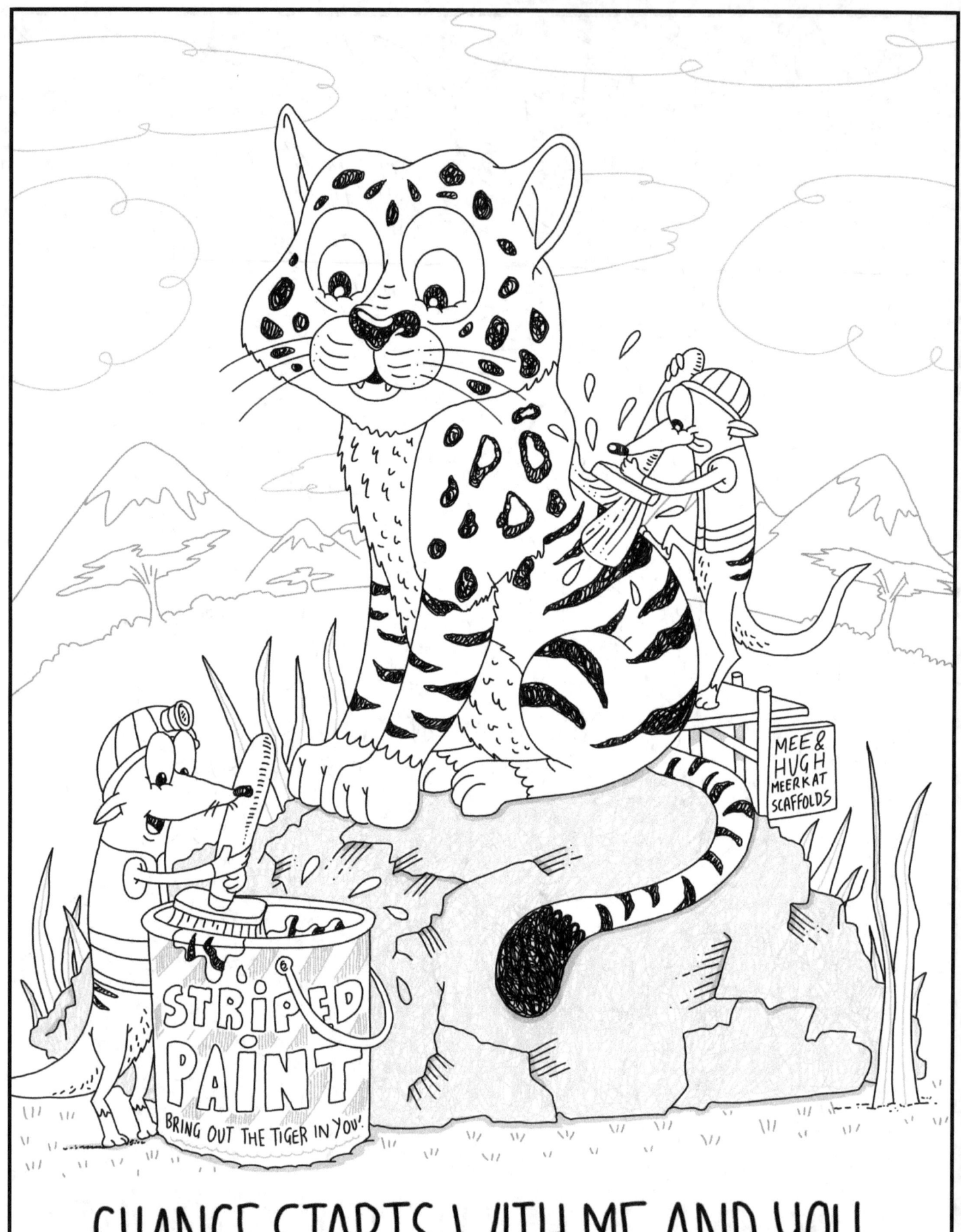

CHANGE STARTS WITH ME AND YOU

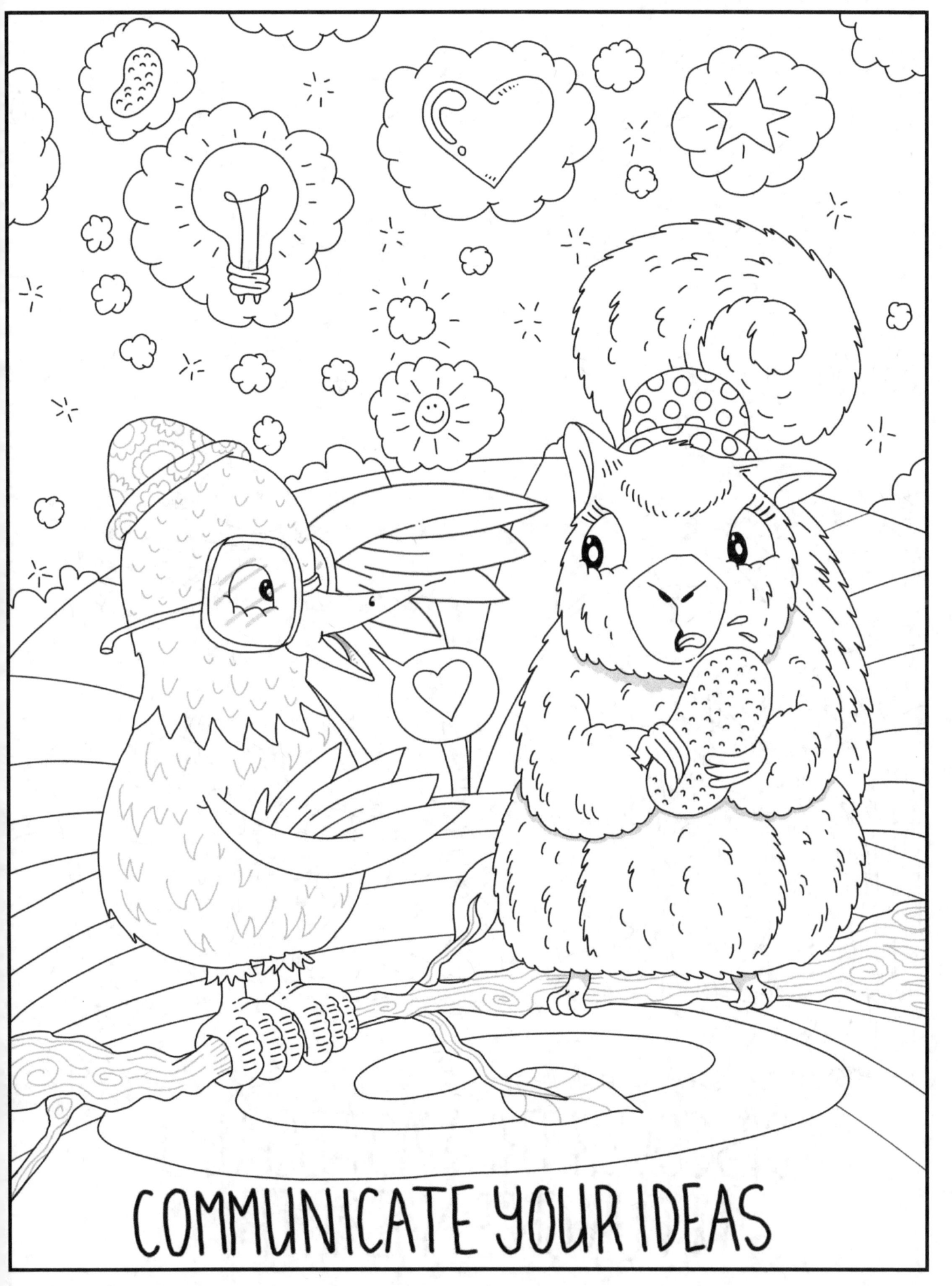

COMMUNICATE YOUR IDEAS

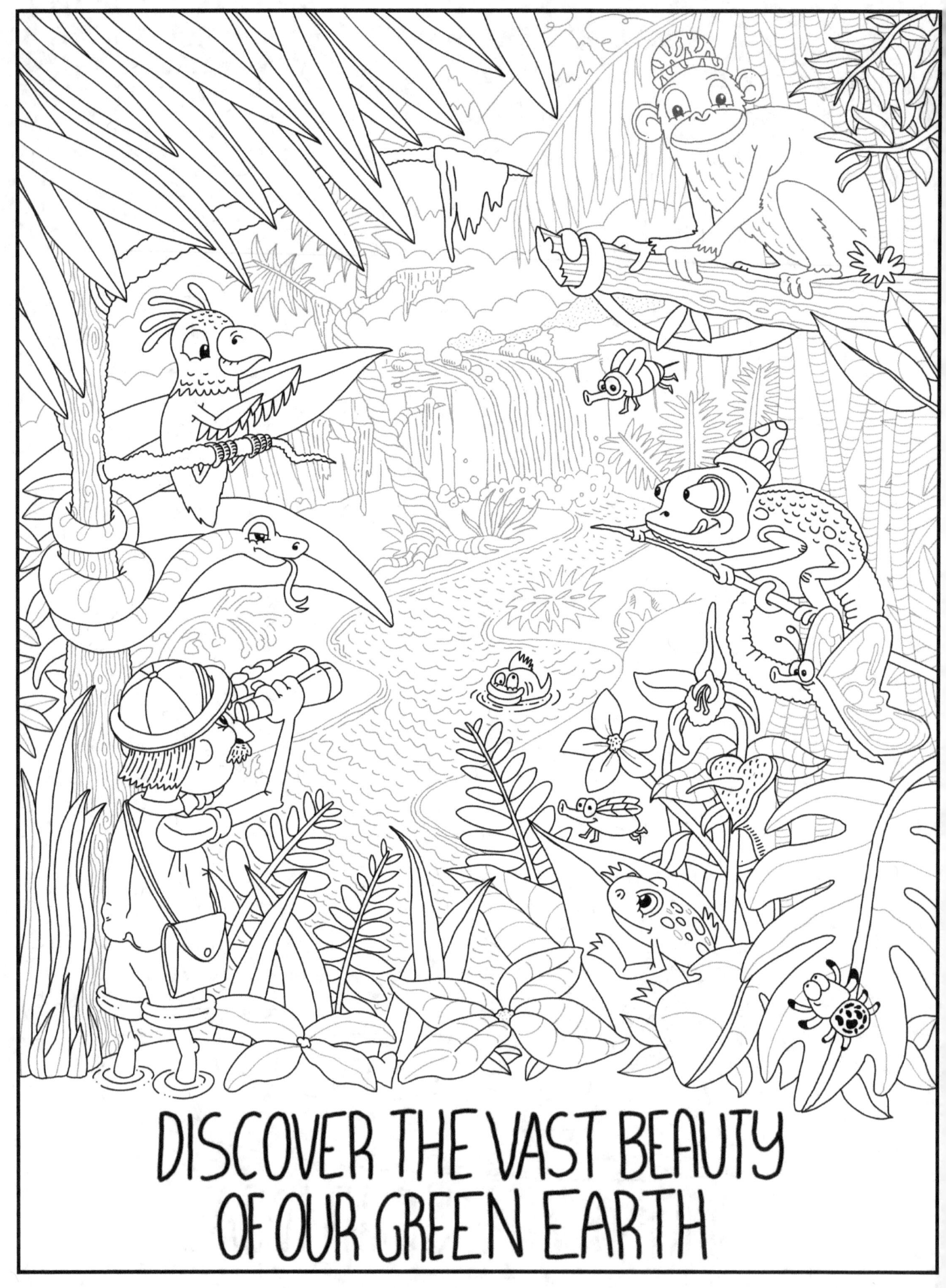

DISCOVER THE VAST BEAUTY
OF OUR GREEN EARTH

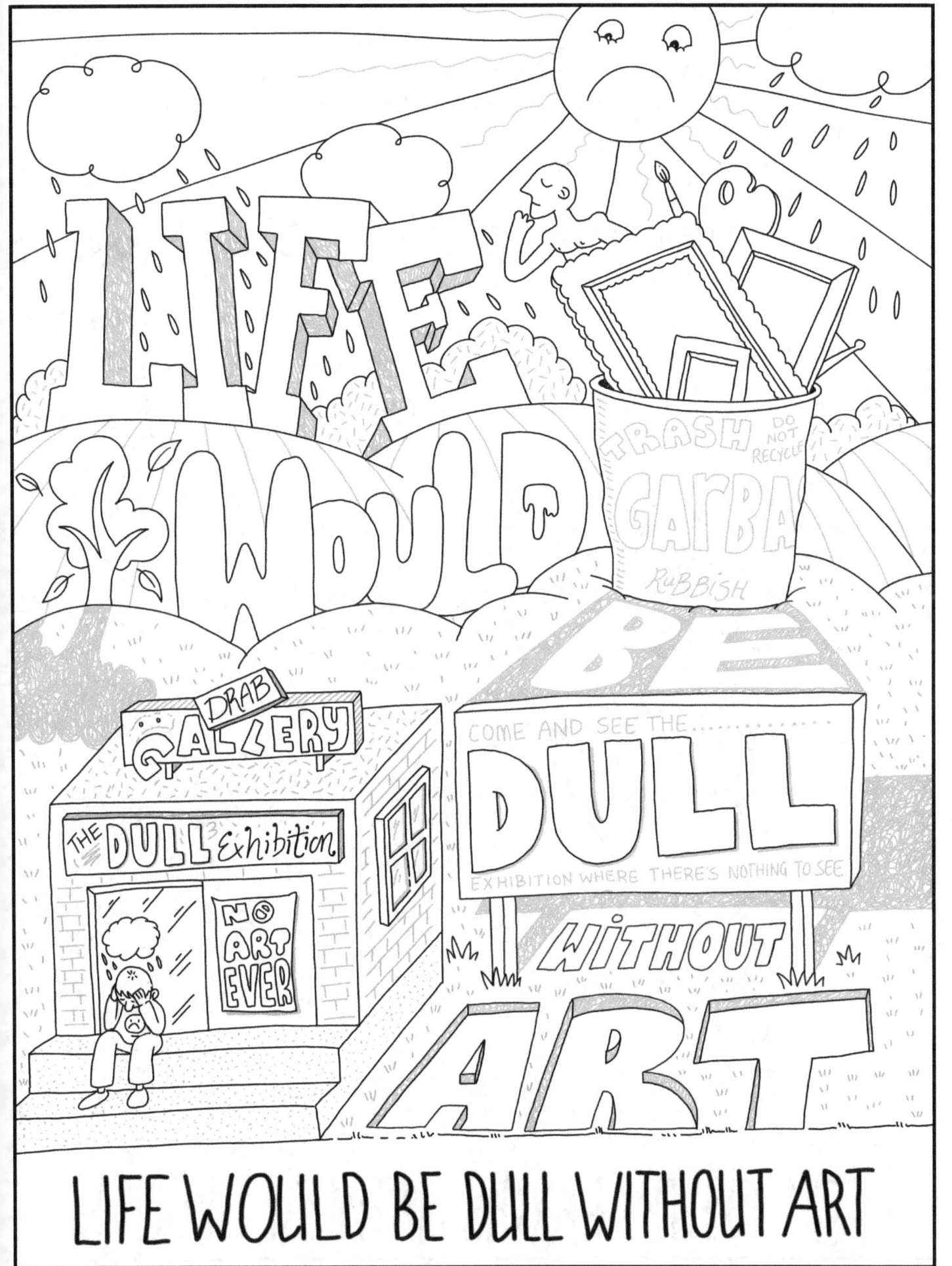

LIFE WOULD BE DULL WITHOUT ART

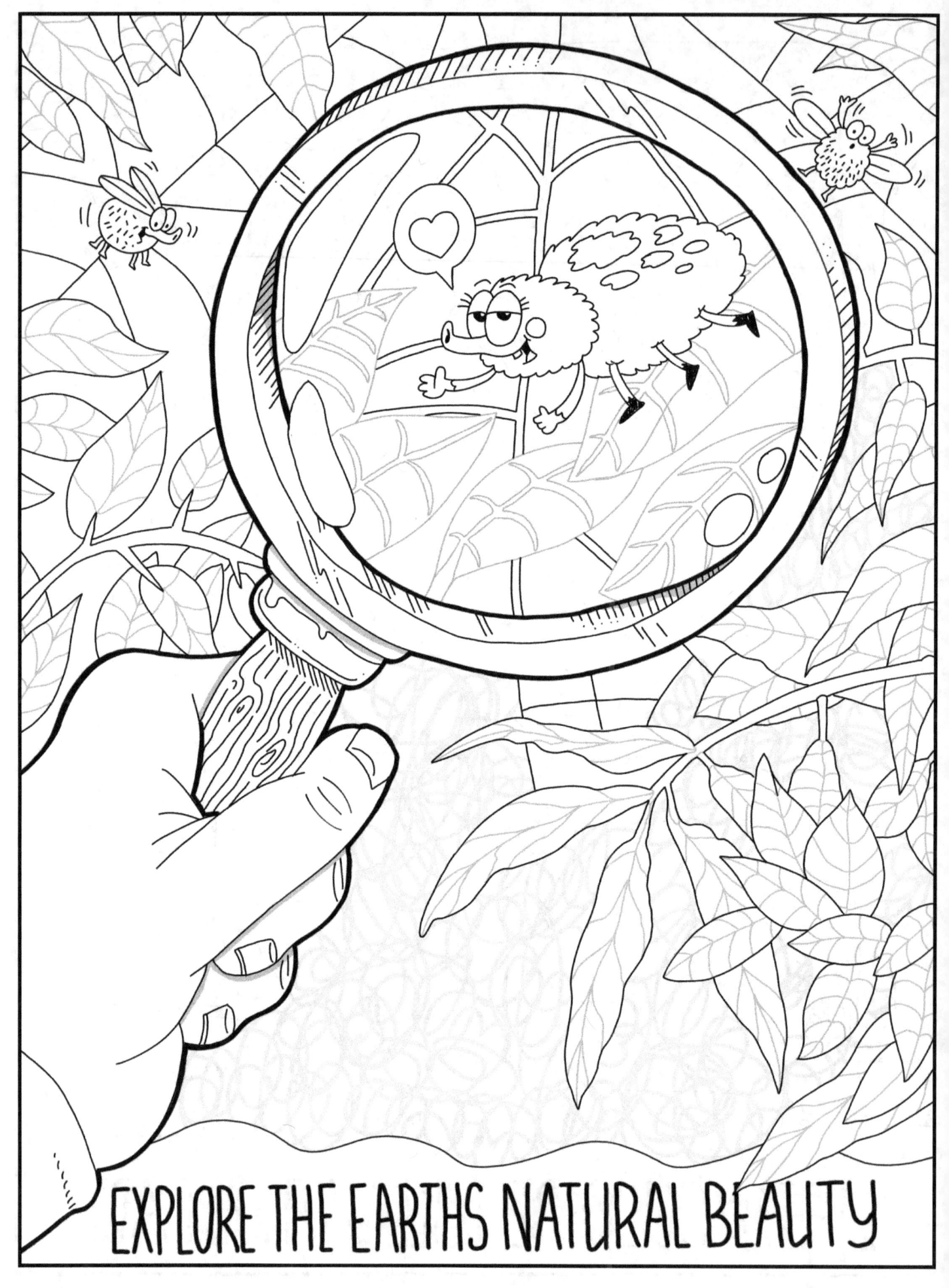

EXPLORE THE EARTHS NATURAL BEAUTY

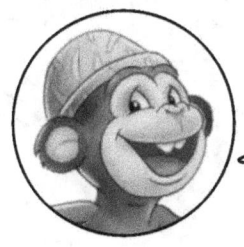

"Hello, I'm The Doodle Monkey, I love doodling fruit. Like my friend Eric the Banana.
I have an awesome idea! You could doodle your favorite fruits and share it with someone you love to color"

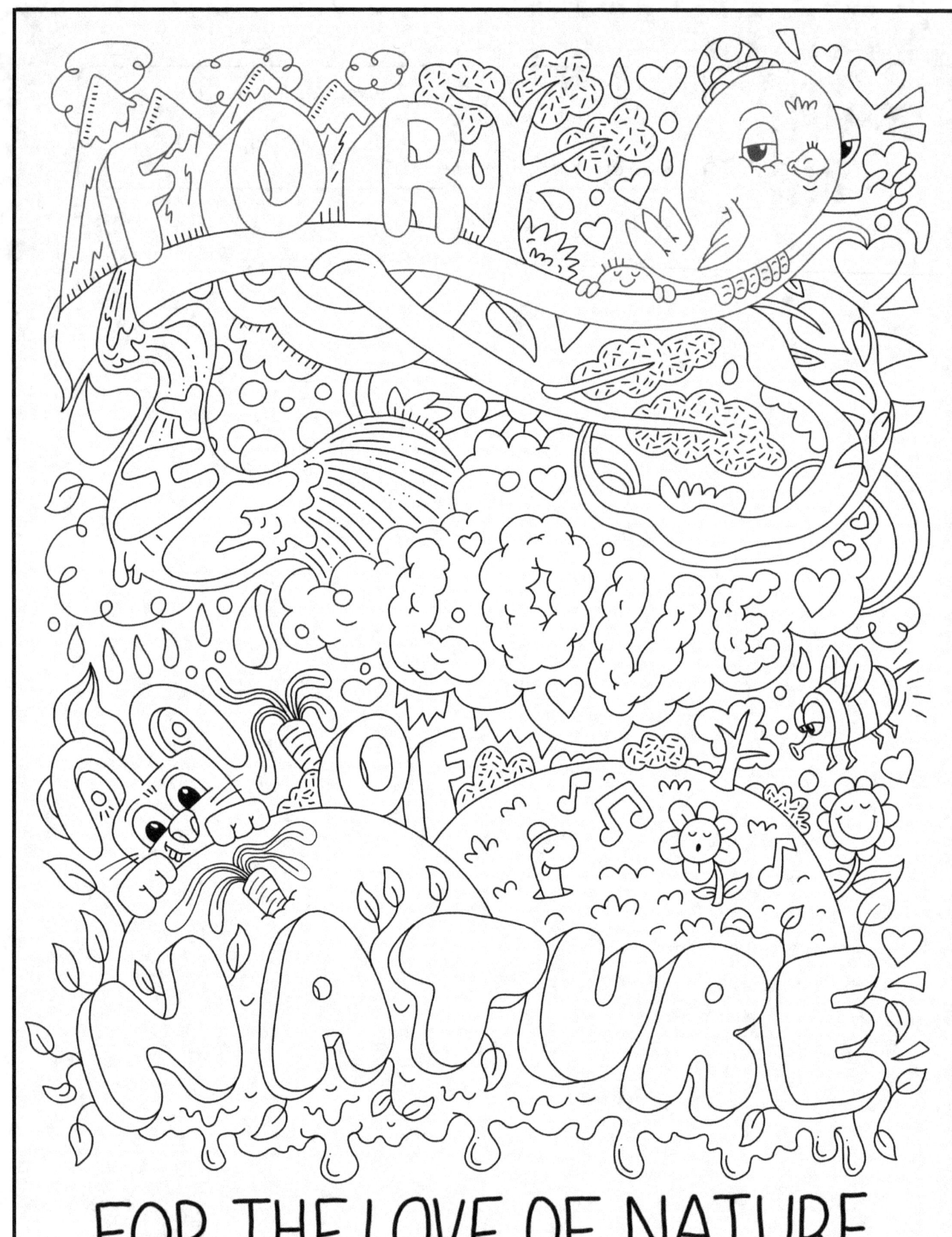

FOR THE LOVE OF NATURE

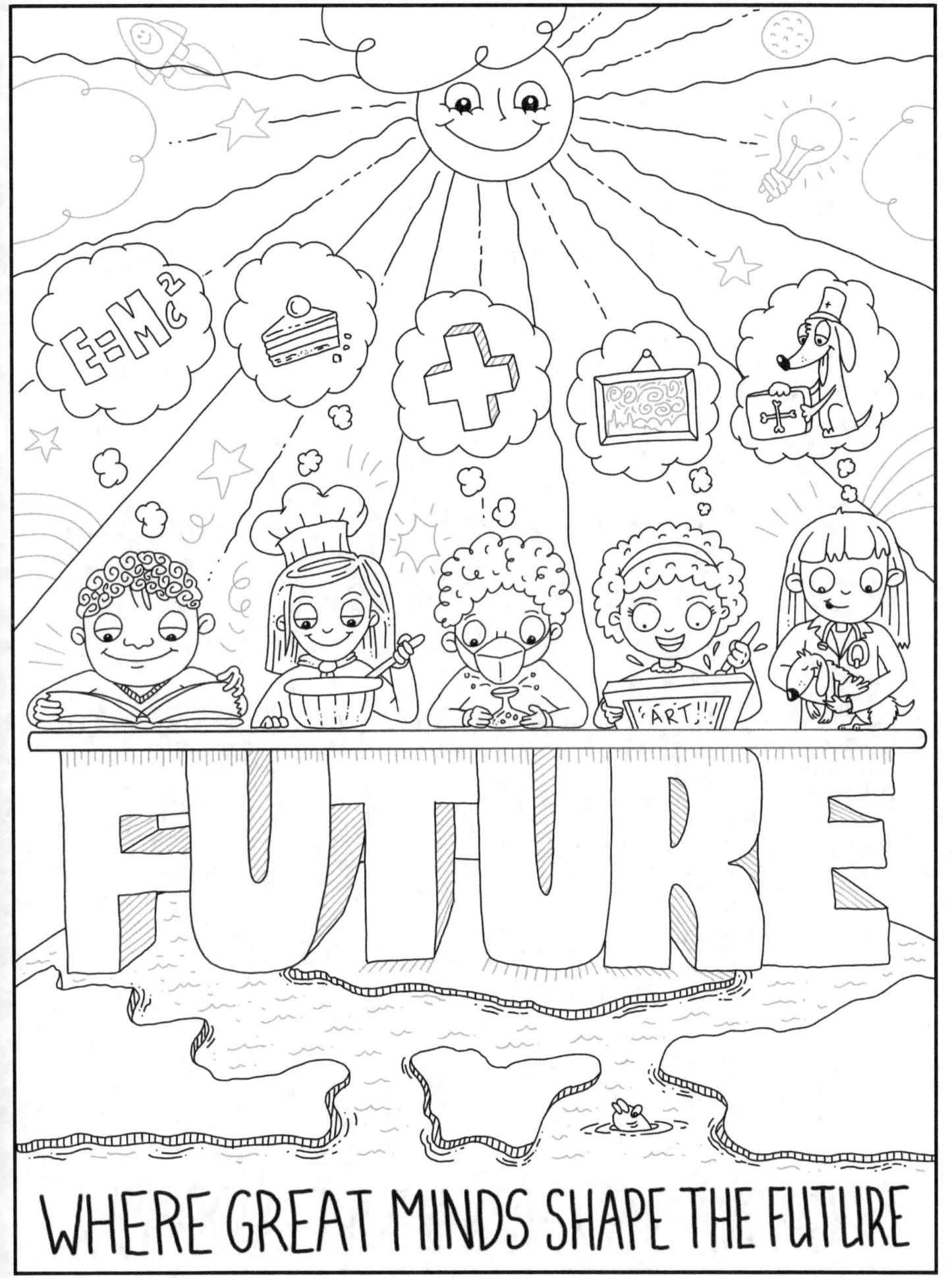

WHERE GREAT MINDS SHAPE THE FUTURE

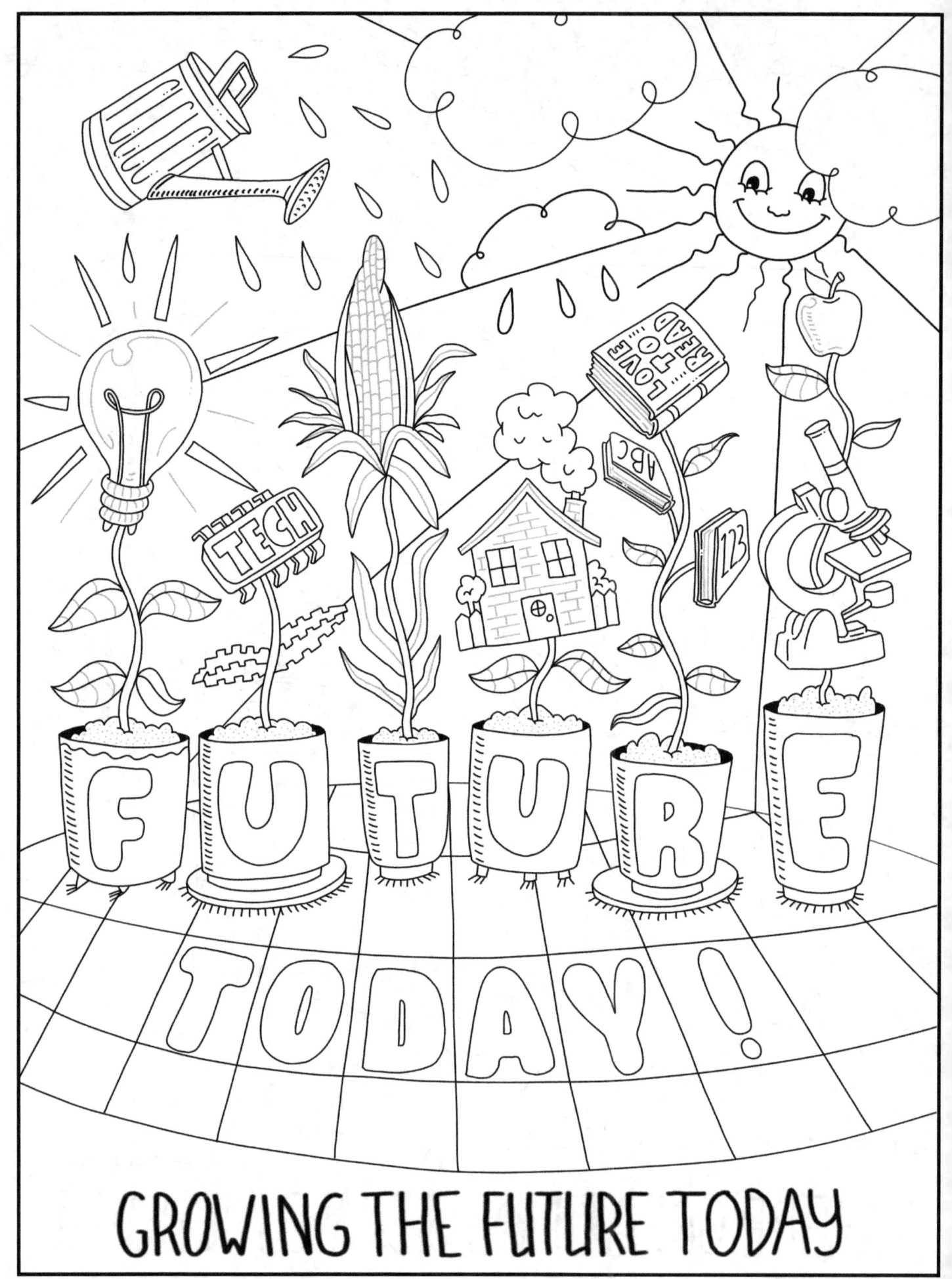

GROWING THE FUTURE TODAY

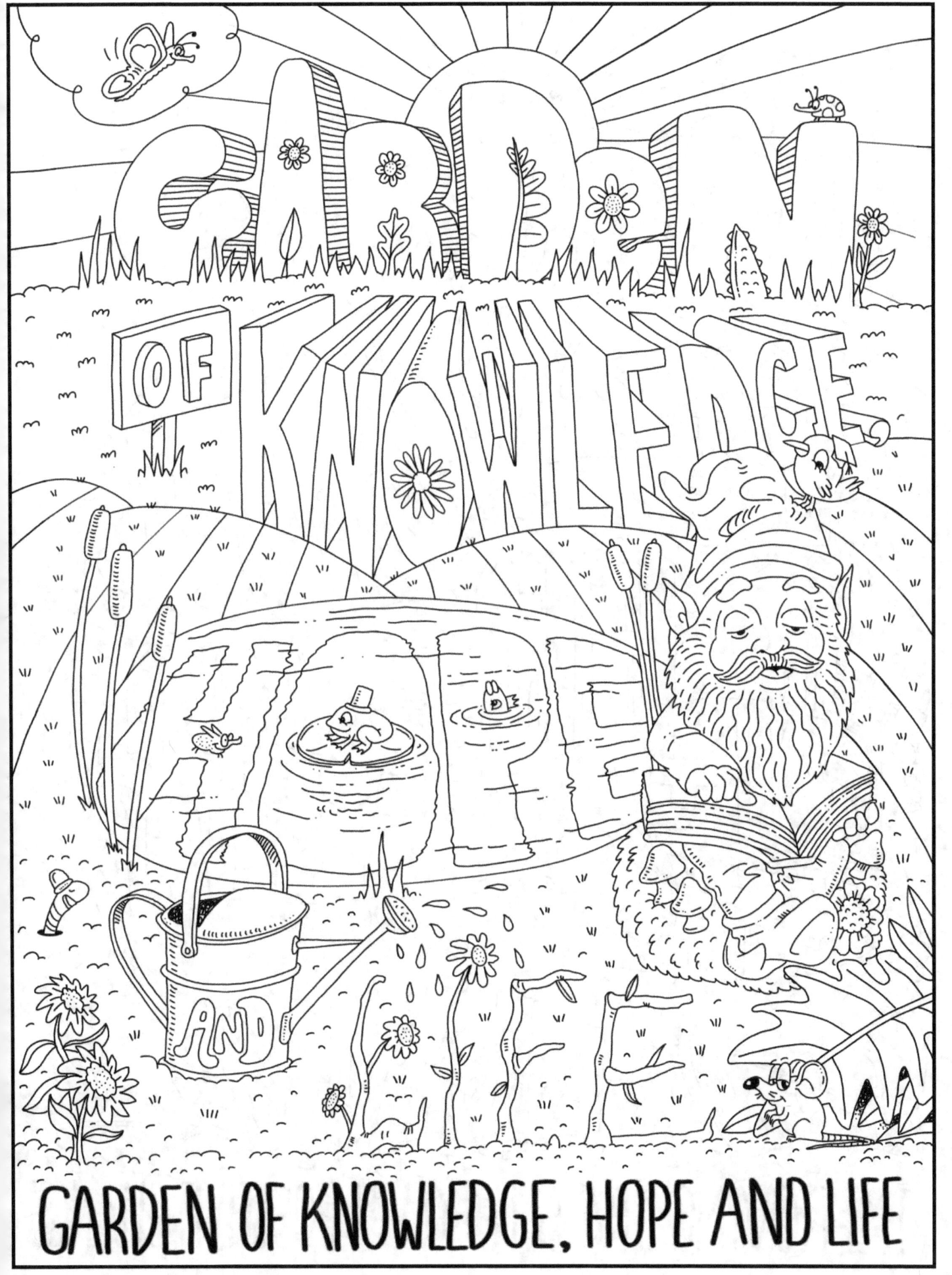

GARDEN OF KNOWLEDGE, HOPE AND LIFE

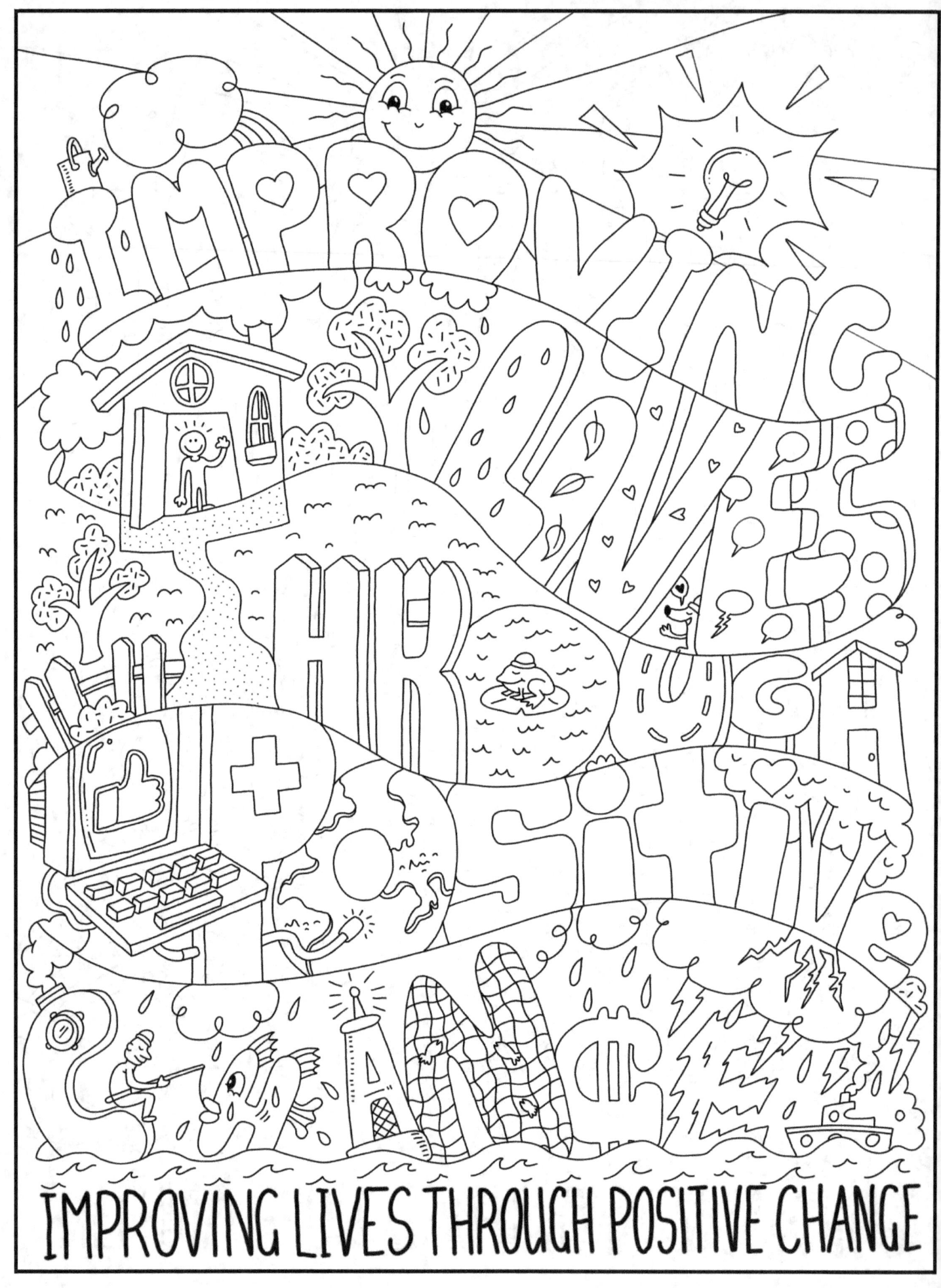

IMPROVING LIVES THROUGH POSITIVE CHANGE

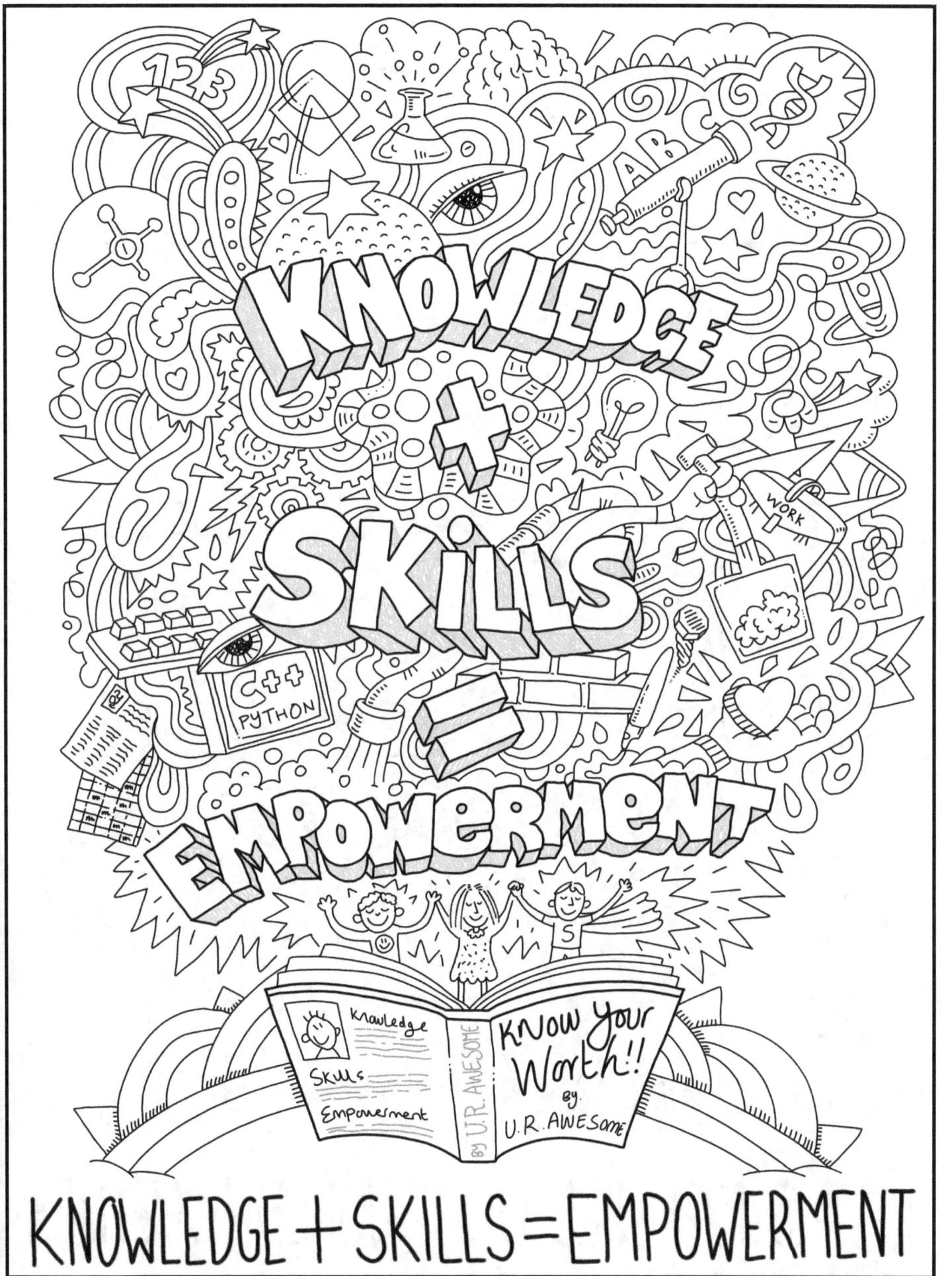

KNOWLEDGE + SKILLS = EMPOWERMENT

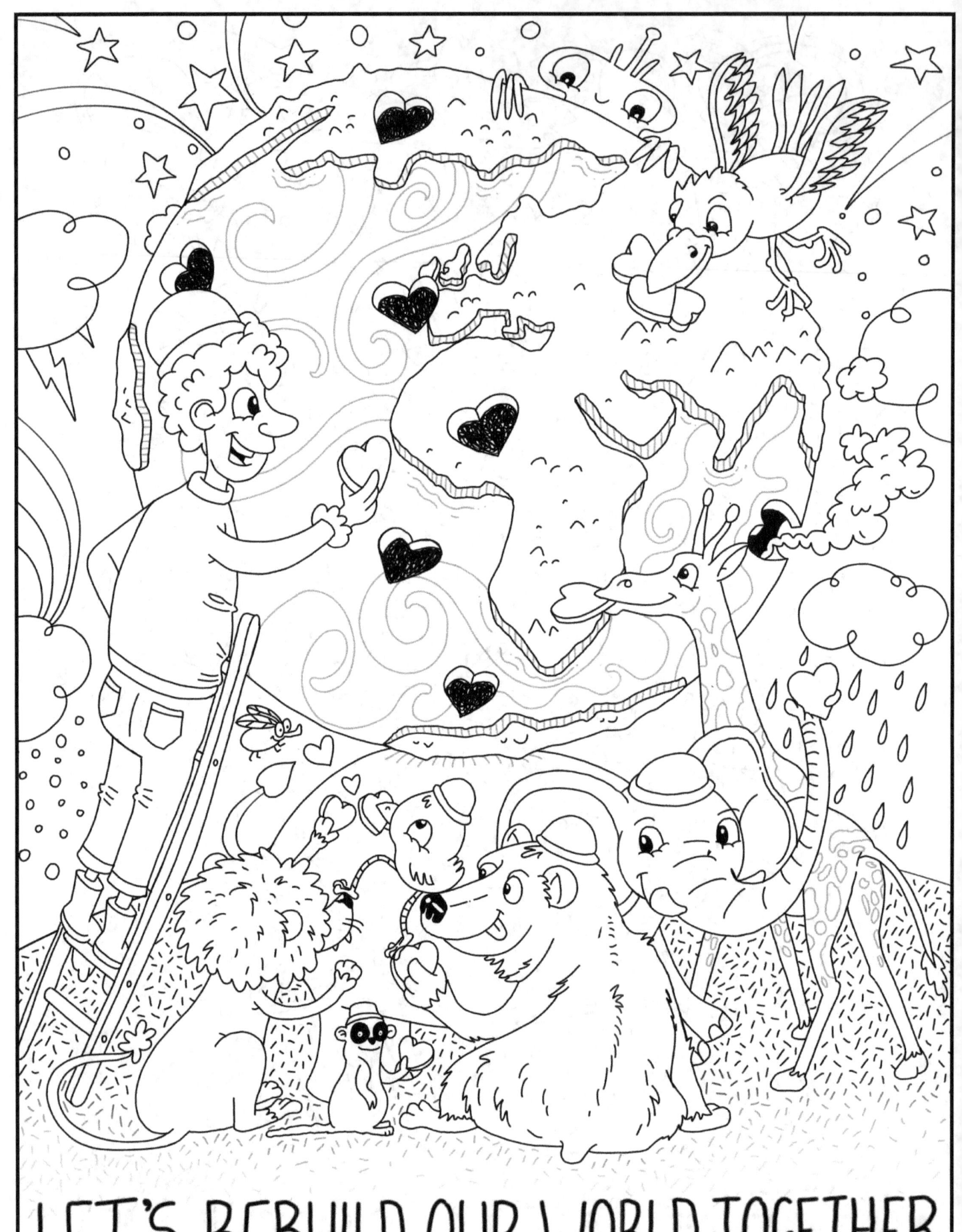

LET'S REBUILD OUR WORLD TOGETHER

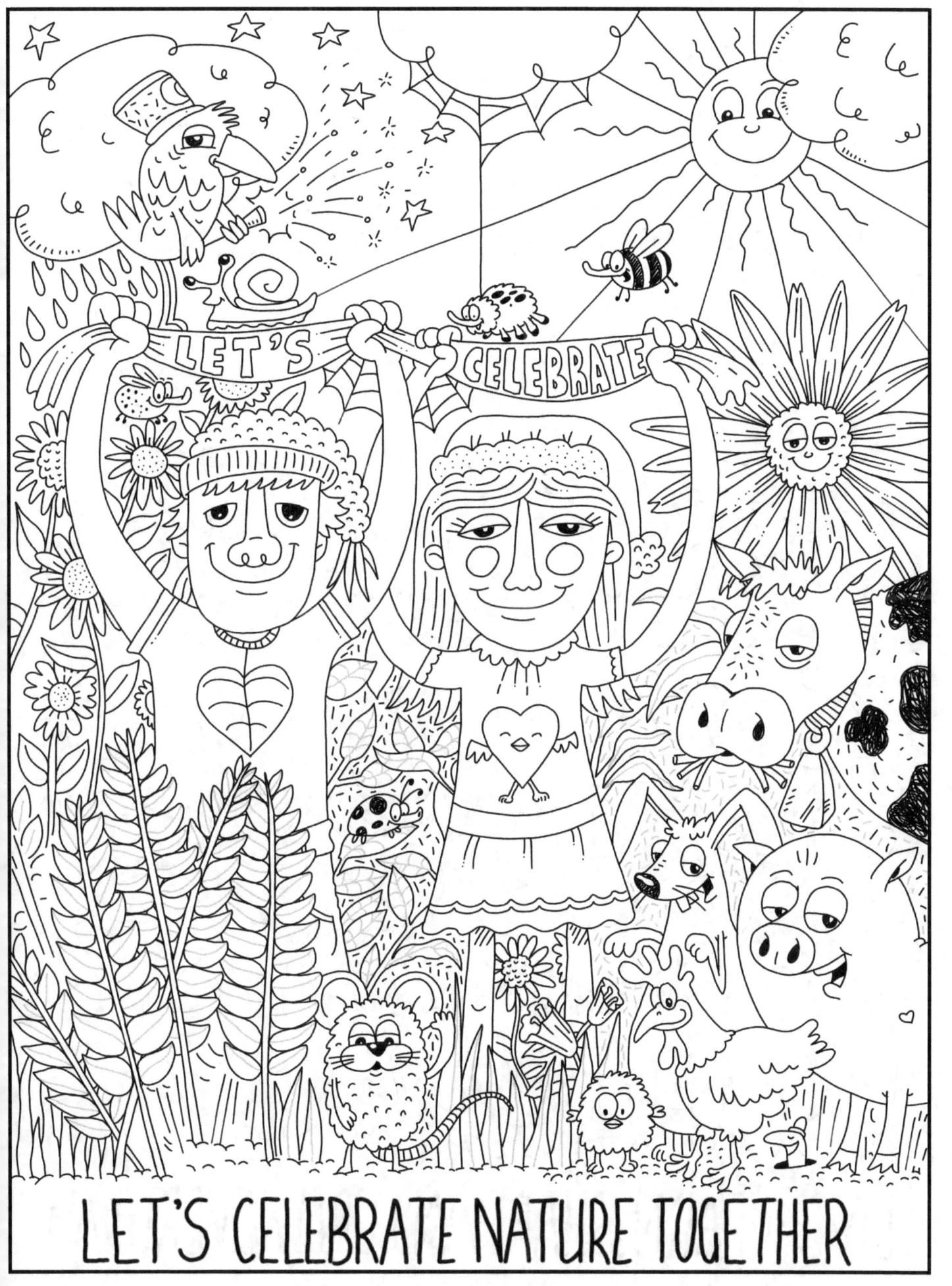

LET'S CELEBRATE NATURE TOGETHER

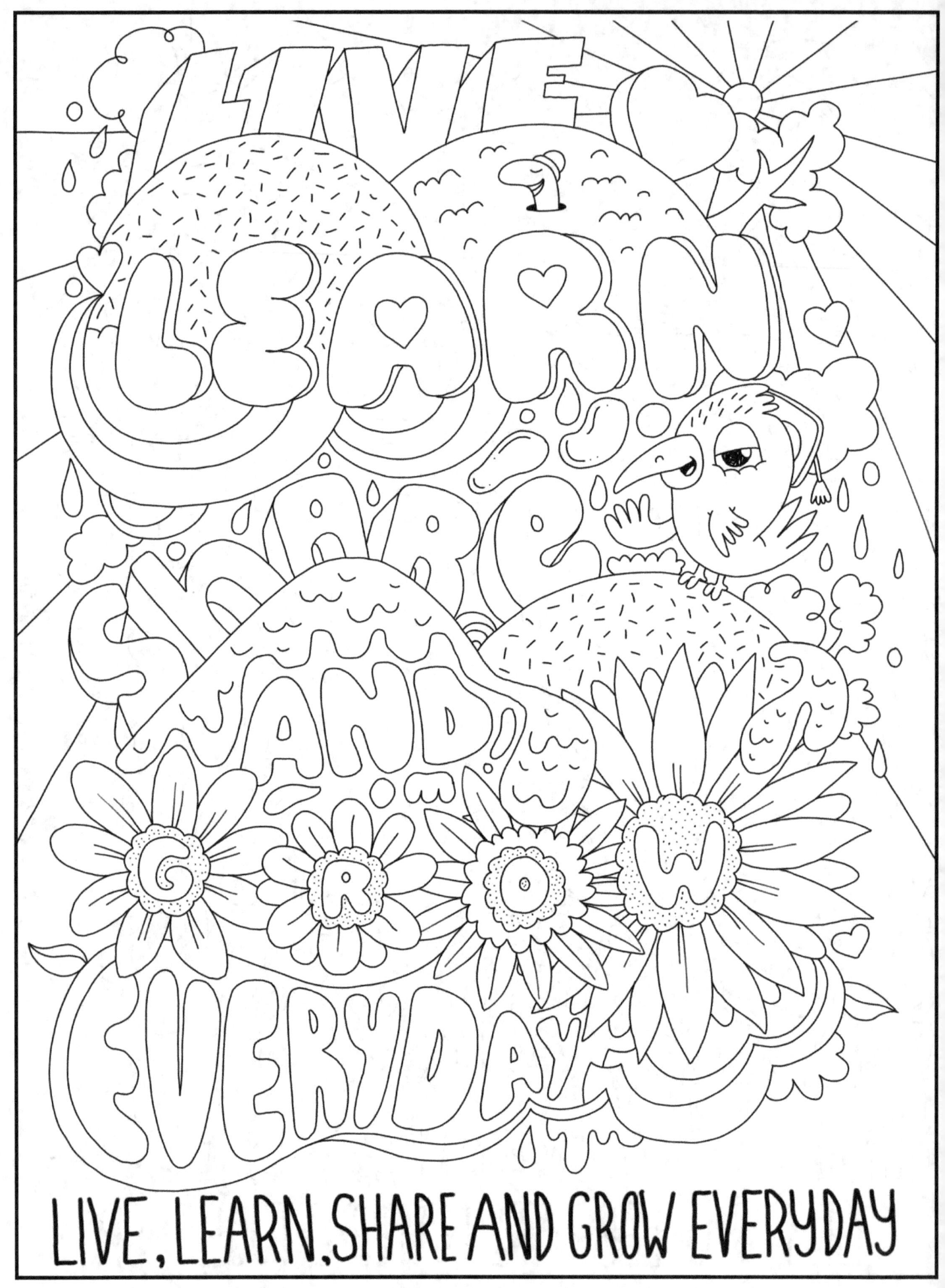

LIVE, LEARN, SHARE AND GROW EVERYDAY

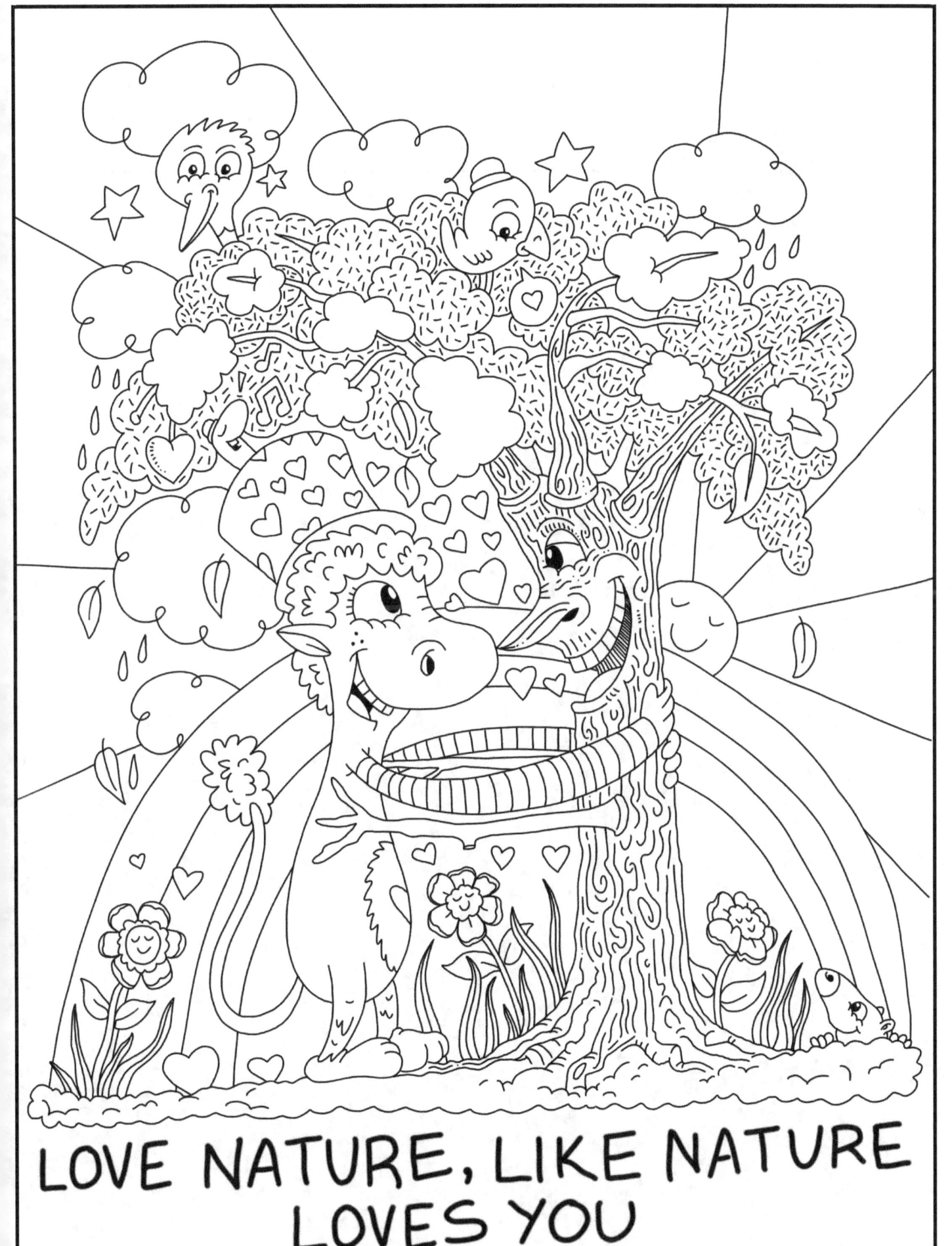

LOVE NATURE, LIKE NATURE
LOVES YOU

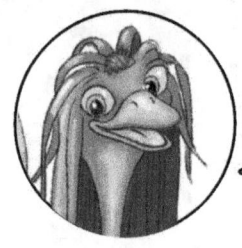

"Hello! I'm Frieburd, I love creating drawings of beautiful nature, such as, flowers, trees, birds, animals and insects. I would love to see your drawings of nature."

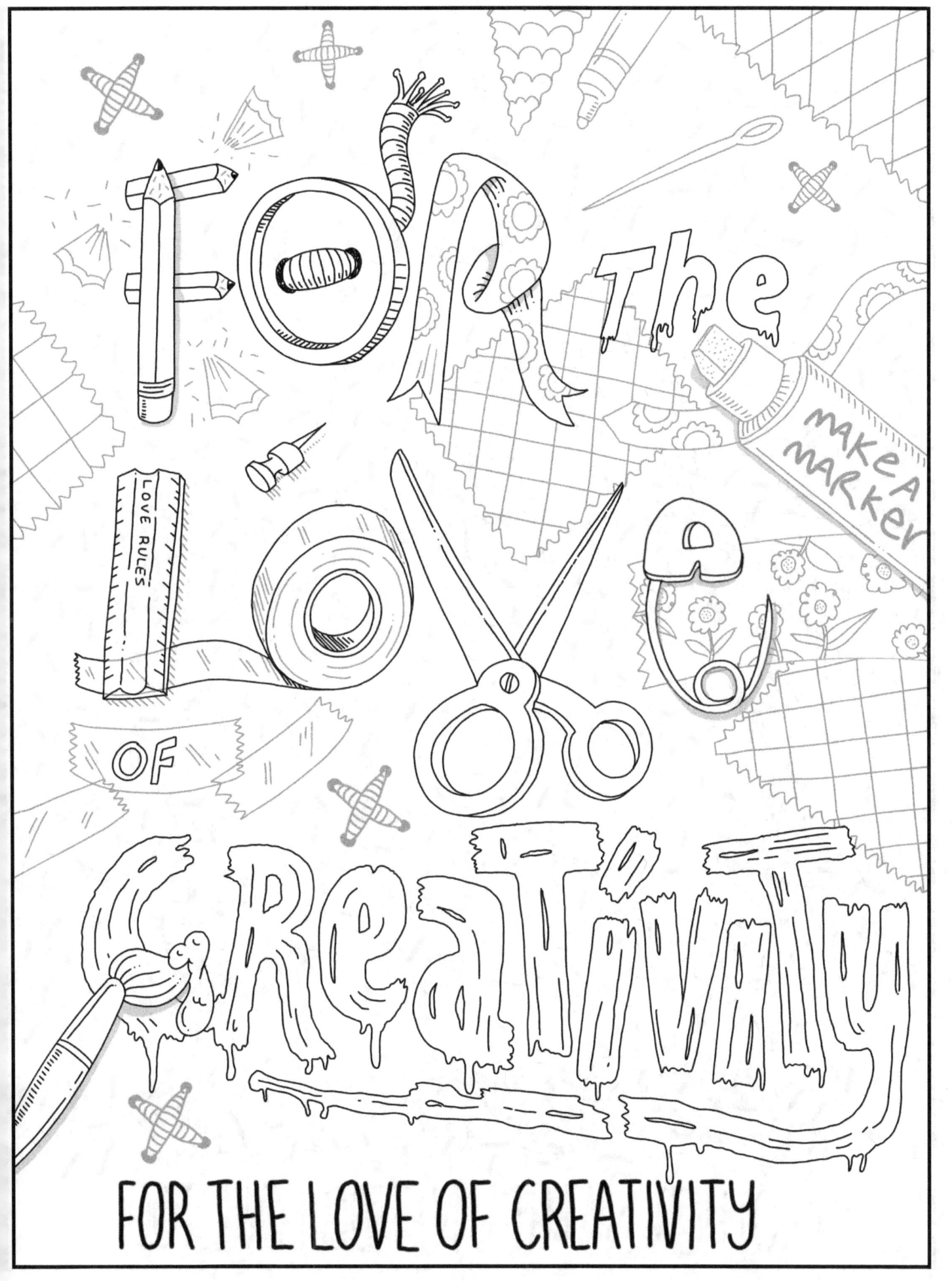

FOR THE LOVE OF CREATIVITY

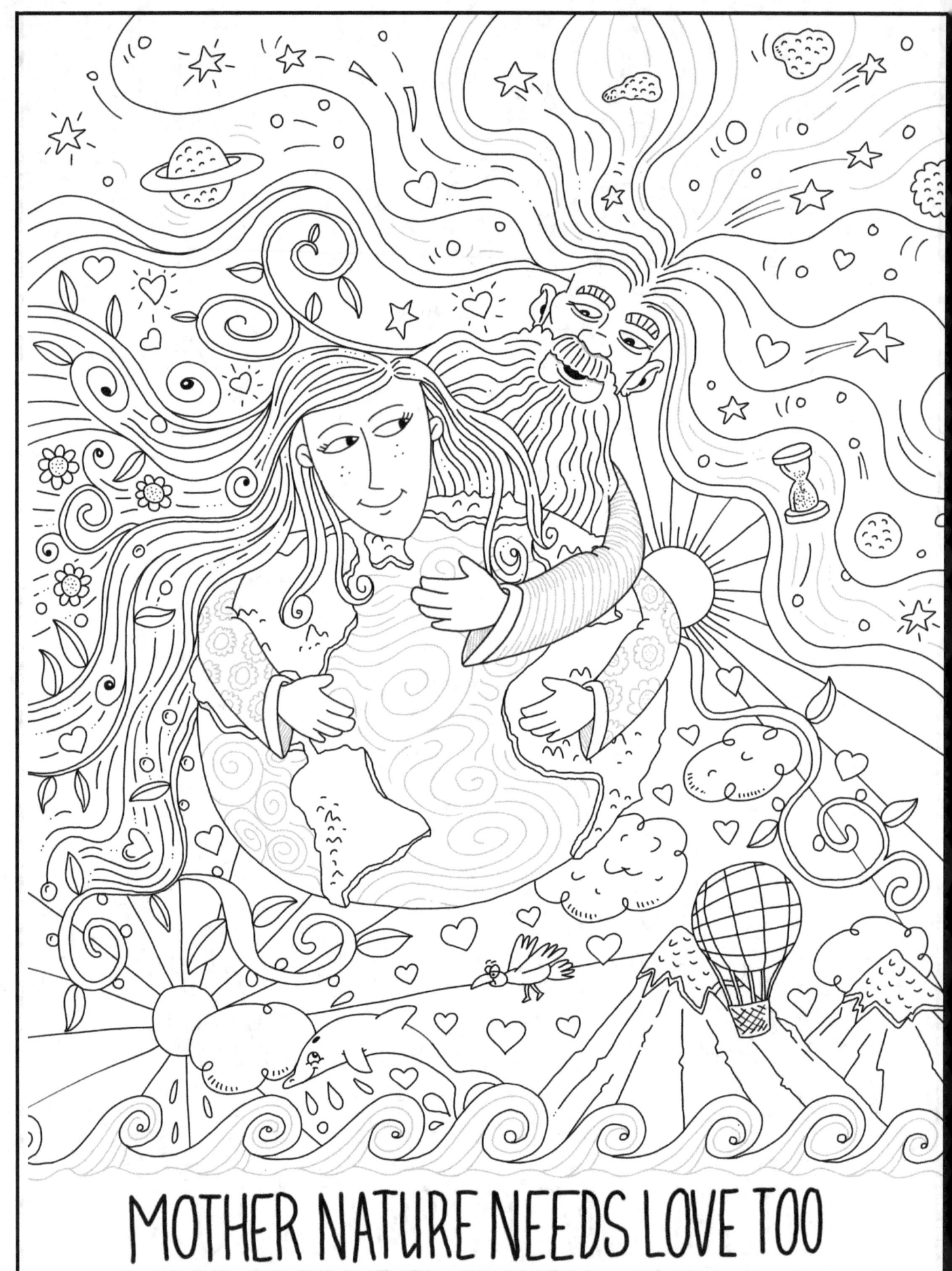

MOTHER NATURE NEEDS LOVE TOO

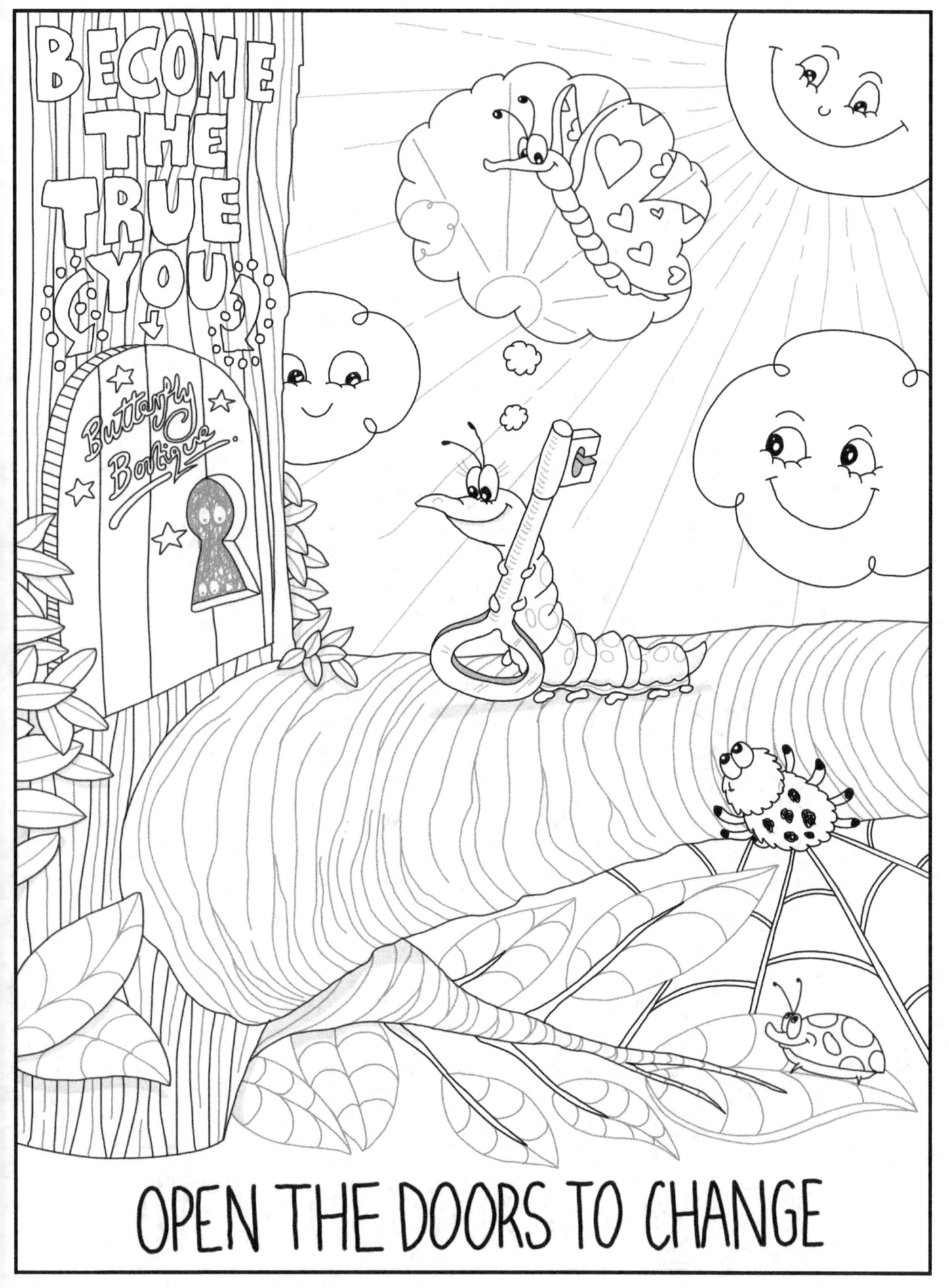

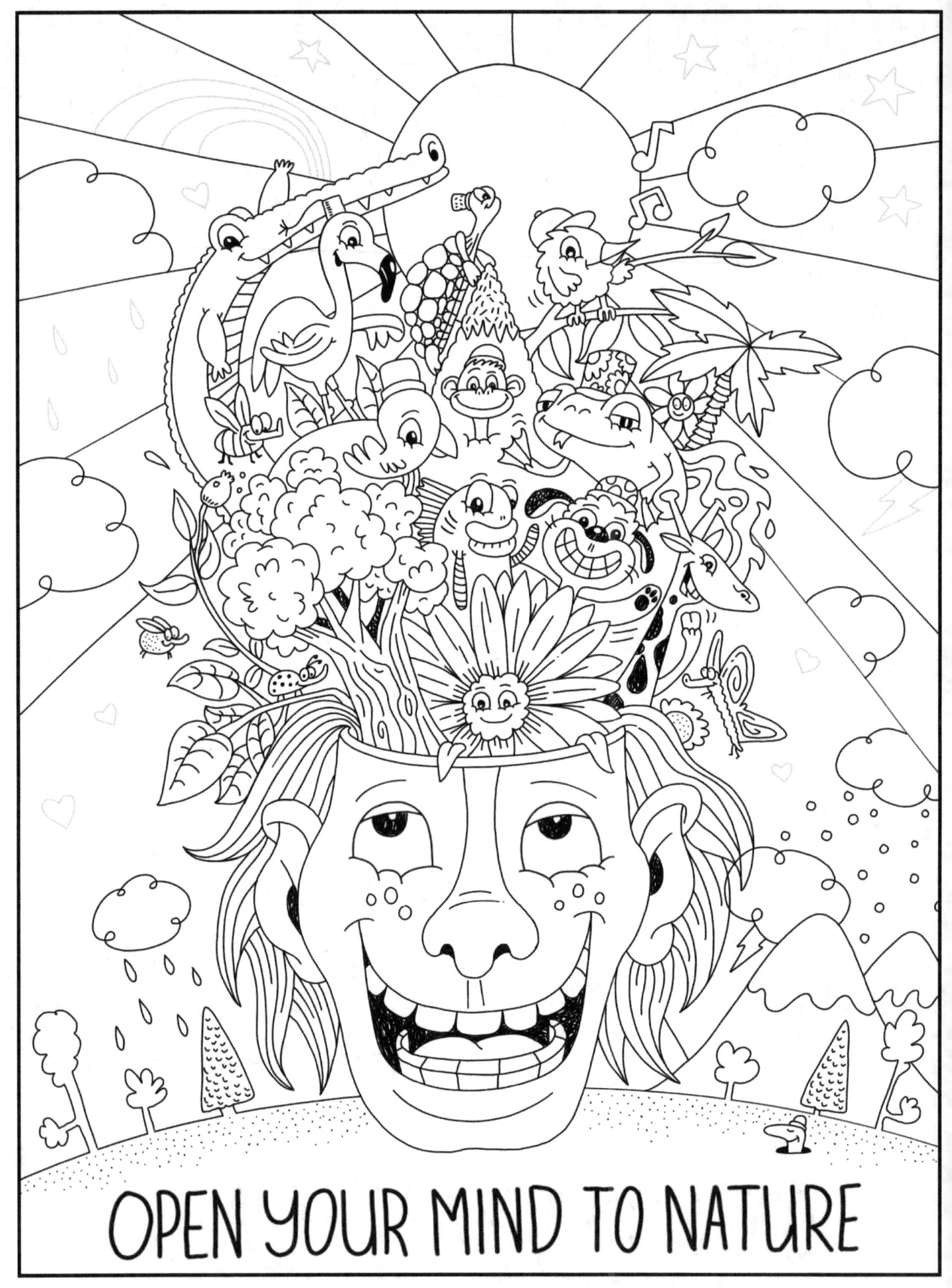

OPEN YOUR MIND TO NATURE

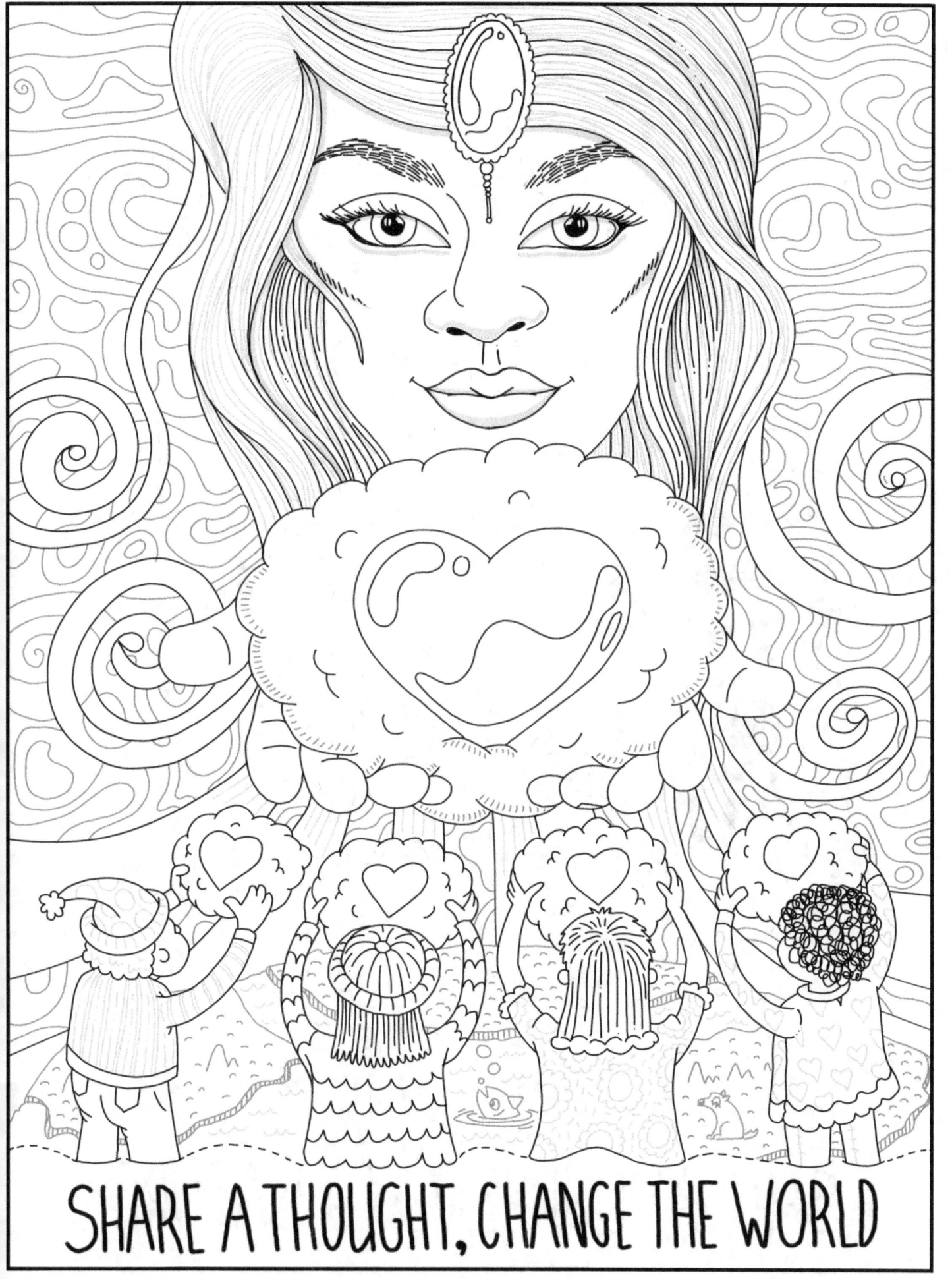

SHARE A THOUGHT, CHANGE THE WORLD

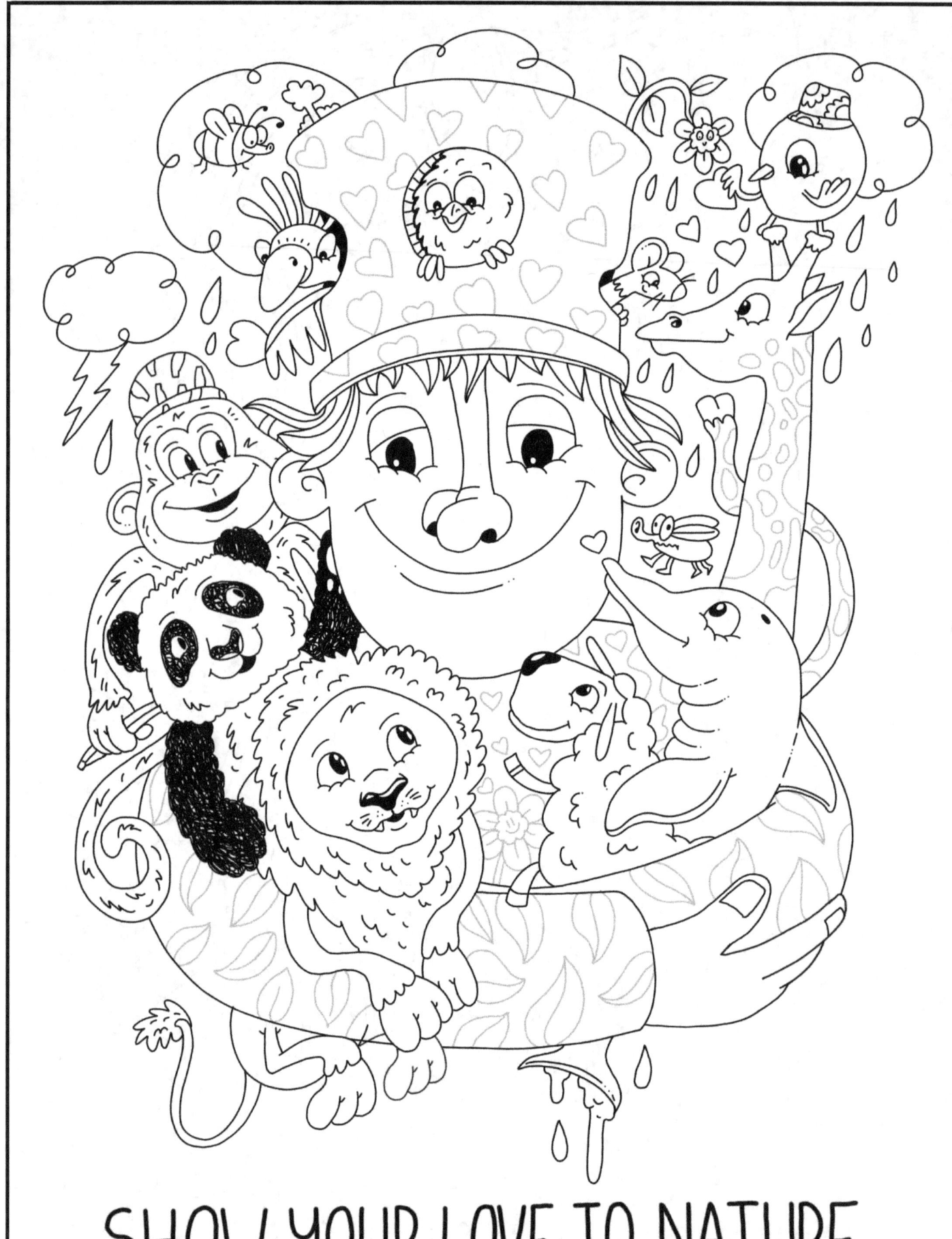

SHOW YOUR LOVE TO NATURE

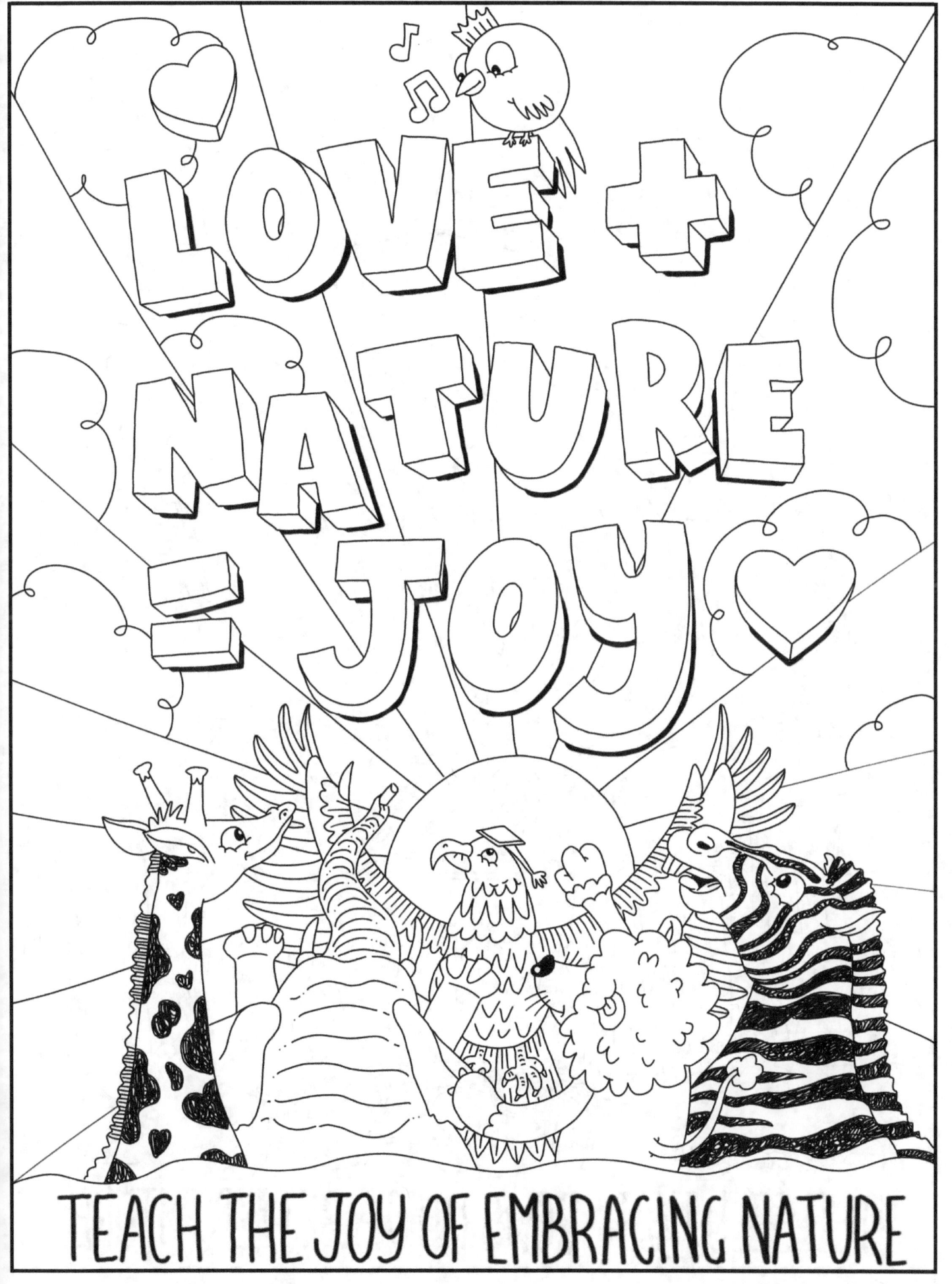

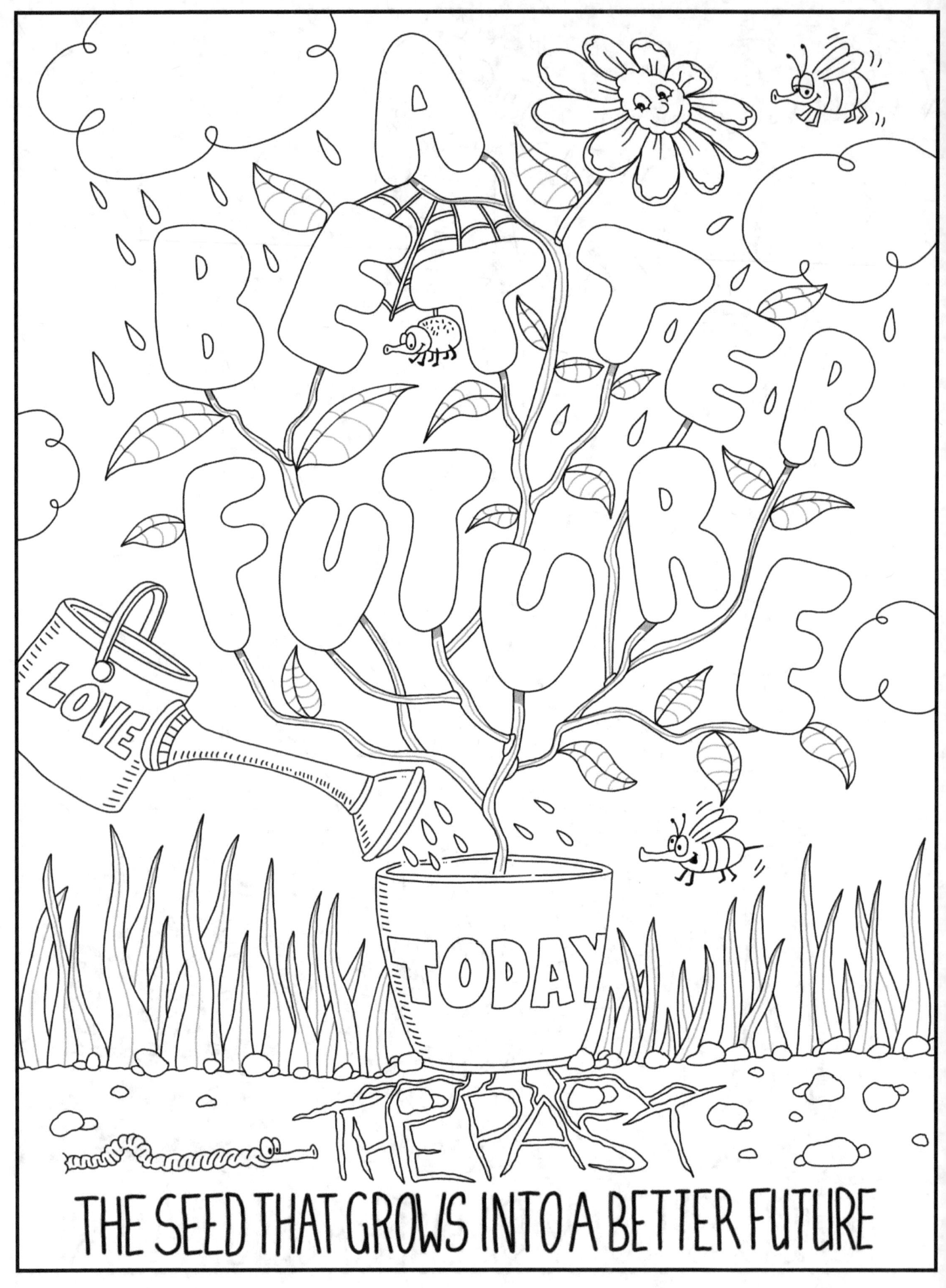

THE SEED THAT GROWS INTO A BETTER FUTURE

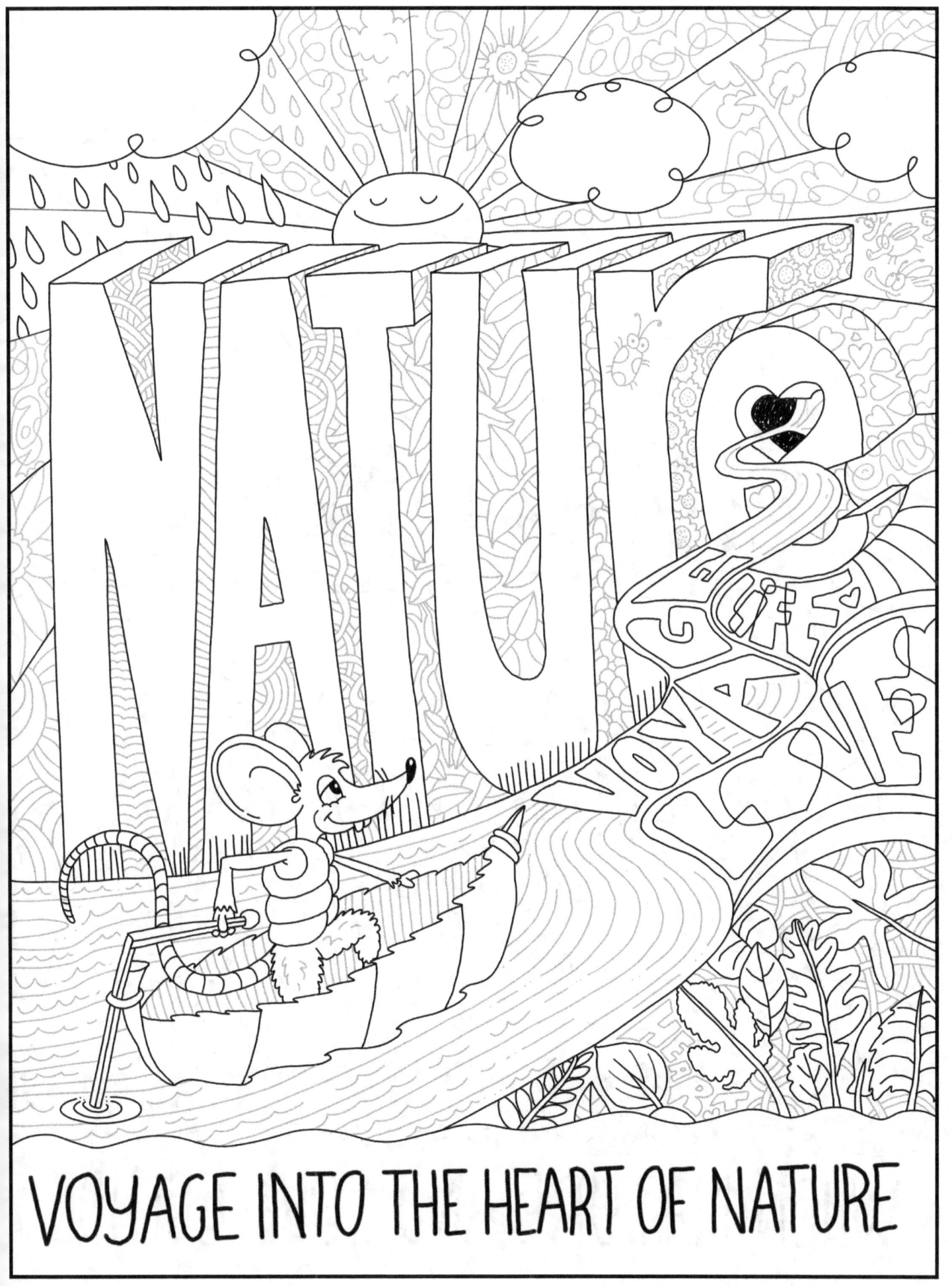

VOYAGE INTO THE HEART OF NATURE

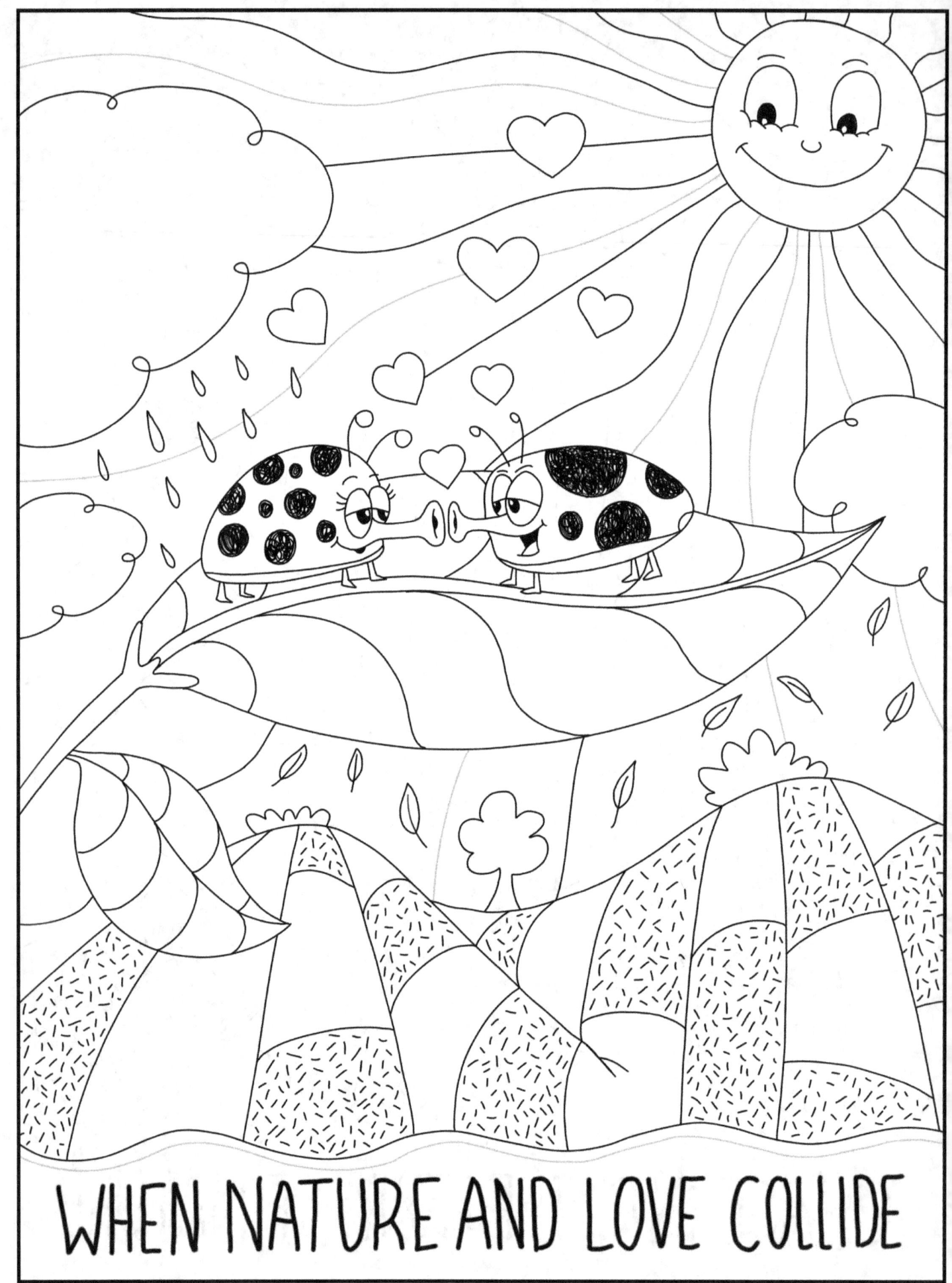

WHEN NATURE AND LOVE COLLIDE

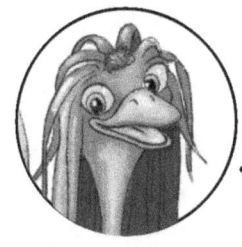

"Hi, it's me again, your friendly neighborhood FrieBurd. I was just thinking ... if you're loving doodling and drawing, why not go into the garden and draw some awesome things from nature."